Marek J. Murawski

Messerschmitt Bf 109 T
the Luftwaffe's Naval Fighter

KAGERO

Contents

Introduction 3

"Graf Zeppelin" and her aircraft 6

Operational service 21

In the new role over the North Sea 31

Bibliography 50

Endnotes 50

Appendices 51

Acknowledgements:
The author would like to express his gratitude to the following persons, who kindly helped in creating this book: Tomasz Szlagor, Janusz Światłoń, Arkadiusz Wróbel, Hans J. Nowarra (+) oraz Bernd Barbas

Messerschmitt Bf 109 T – the Luftwaffe's Naval Fighter • Marek J. Murawski
First edition • LUBLIN 2007

ISBN 978-83-60445-83-9

© All rights reserved. With the exception of quoting brief passages for the purposes of review, no part of this publication may be reproduced without prior written permission from the Publisher.

Editing: **Marek J. Murawski**
Translation: **Tomasz Szlagor**
Cover artwork: **Arkadiusz Wróbel**
Color profiles: **Janusz Światłoń**
Scale drawings: **Mariusz Łukasik**
Design: **Tomasz Gąska, KAGERO STUDIO**

Oficyna Wydawnicza KAGERO
www.kagero.pl • e-mail: kagero@kagero.pl, marketing@kagero.pl

Editorial office, Marketing, Distribution:
OW KAGERO, ul. Mełgiewska 7-9, 20-952 Lublin
tel.: (+48) 081 749 20 20, tel./fax (+48) 081 749 11 81, www.kagero.pl

A damaged B-17 Flying Fortress. *(Michael Koenig)*

The 'weather frog'[1] had forecast that weather conditions would improve. Everything went as I had thought it would: first, the warning; then combat readiness and an 'alarm-start' take-off -all part of the routine. However, the first wave of enemy aircraft suddenly turned back and we were ordered to return to base. It seemed to be a ruse employed by the Americans to wear down our fighter force. If so, it failed to accomplish anything for we immediately re-fuelled and at 11:22 hrs took off again. We were vectored south, where another enemy formation had been detected. At 11:42 hrs our four aircraft made first contact with the enemy in the vicinity of Cuxhaven, at 6500 meters. We overtook the Americans and at 11:44 hrs swerved around for a head-on attack. Unfortunately, we did it too early – and before we could close in, the enemy formation changed course, spoiling our attack. Only two of our machines were properly lined up. Our Schwarm[2] reformed and again we raced for the head of the bomber formation.

It took a considerable amount of time because the Americans were flying quite fast. On this occasion our timing was better and as we whipped around, each of us was well positioned. I was flying the No 3 slot, as the leader of the second pair, behind the Schwarmführer and his Katschmarek[3]. Six hundred meters to go… five hundred… We were charging headlong into a Pulk[4] of 35 heavy bombers, closing the distance at a combined speed of 1,000 kph. I thumbed the machine gun trigger. The nose of 'my' Boeing was centered in the crosshairs of my Revi gunsight, illuminated on the windshield. At 300 meters the Boeing's wings filled the horizontal reticle of my sight. I squeezed the triggers. My guns ripped out three short bursts. I could see a hail of projectiles hitting the bomber's wings and engines. I pushed the stick forward to pass below the stricken bomber. Its gunners opened up on me with all they had, but it was already too late for them. I hauled back on the stick, rolled to port and watched the drama unfold below me. The Boeing pulled sharply up, leaving a trail of white smoke – then tipped over to starboard and spun down. Its right wing and engines were aflame. I saw two crew members bail out. A moment later the bomber broke apart, and the burning debris fell into the sea between the Wangerooge and Heligoland islands. I yelled 'Sieg Heil!' into the microphone and heard others from my Schwarm congratulate me: but our battle was not over yet. Only then did I notice that an explosive round had blasted through my right wing; howev-

Many B-17s intercepted by German fighters ended up in the North Sea. *(Michael Koenig)*

er, my machine still handled pretty well. I spotted a Boeing in a wide turn and, with the advantage of height, bore in from the rear. Again, I saw the flashes of my impacting rounds. The bomber's return fire was waning. My second and third passes went unopposed. I closed in to 50 meters and again blazed away. The Fortress was losing height and straggling behind the formation, but still flying. When I engaged for the fourth time, my guns remained silent – I had run out of ammunition. I then moved to the side of the bomber and waggled my wings to inform the pilot that I wanted him to turn back and land. In response I was raked with a burst from the bomber's waist gun position. I felt a smack against the engine and a sudden pricking pain in my left arm. When I came to my senses and regained control over my aircraft, I was down to 4,000-5,000 meters. A gush of hot oil spewed back at me from the battered engine and poured into my flying boots. I could barely see outside the cockpit. The left sleeve of my jacket was torn. I felt a burning pain but could still use my left hand. The bullet had merely grazed the muscles of my arm and the wound was superficial. Had it strayed some eight centimeters to the left, it would have hit me in the heart.

The oil gauge showed zero. I could not throttle up for fear of killing the engine. I resolved to semi-glide towards Heligoland, some 20 kilometers away. I needed some power from the failing engine to get to the island. I readied myself to bail out, but at the same time I strove to maintain as much altitude as possible; 3000 meters, 2000, 1000… My crippled machine was steadily losing height. I hesitated. There was still time to take to my parachute. The airstrip at the island was short. If I miscalculated my approach, I would fall into the sea, slam into the pier or nose over.

Whether the jump seemed too risky or I was afraid of the water, I don't know. Either way, I headed straight for the concrete runway and, using the last burst of power from the engine, I touched down. As I did so the engine quit and I merely rolled down the runway. I tried to brake but the hydraulic installation in the right wheel was also shot up. My 'Toni'[5] veered to port and wobbled towards other aircraft parked in their revetments. At last, it came to a stop only ten meters distant from them. My skin was damp – I had broken into a cold sweat. I clambered out of the cockpit drenched in oil. My ground crew helped me remove my life vest and fur-lined boots. Dressed only in my shirt, trousers and socks, I trudged towards my billet. When I had time to check on my aircraft, I discovered that an explosive round had struck the starboard cannon barrel; there was a hole in the right wing caused by a 12 mm projectile and the right landing gear leg was shot up. Further examination revealed a three-centimeter hole on the right side of the oil tank, which allowed me to

Willy Messerschmitt (left) and Hubert Bauer, the head of experimental bureau, at the company office in Augsburg. *(Author)*

track the trajectory of a round which had passed through the tank, damaging some electrical wiring, before penetrating the instrument panel from the inside and finally hitting my left arm.

[...]

I was taken to a first aid station run by the Navy, where my wound was properly dressed. It had been a hell of a day and my nerves were really frayed. Two American airmen, who had bailed out, were brought to Heligoland. They personally confirmed my victory. One of my bursts had hit the bomber's cockpit area and killed all the crewmembers in the front section. Another burst had torn into the wing fuel tank and damaged one of the engines. That was enough to knock it down. Initially, the Americans had laughed at the four Messerschmitts that dared to challenge their 35 'heavies'. However, the smiles were quickly wiped from their faces. They were shot down on their first sortie".[6]

First Bf 109 T prototype, Messerschmitt Bf 109 V-17, D-IYMS, in typical RLM 70/71/65 finish. *(Nowarra)*

"Graf Zeppelin" and her aircraft

The German-British agreement signed on 18th June 1935 allowed the German Reich to construct two aircraft carriers. On 28th December 1936 at Deutscher Werf shipyard in Kiel construction work commenced on a carrier designated "Träger A". Less than two years later, on 8th December 1938, the ship was launched. Her godmother was Helga Gräfin von Brandenstein-Zeppelin, daughter of the famous airship designer Graf Ferdinand Zeppelin. The aircraft carrier was christened after him. The launch ceremony was attended by the Reich's Chancellor Adolf Hitler and Herman Göring, the chief of the Air Ministry and the Luftwaffe. The latter made a speech to the audience of 15,000 spectators. The "Graf Zeppelin" measured 250 meters from stem to stern (the flight deck was 241 m long and 30.7 m wide) and her displacement was estimated at 31,400 GRT. She was propelled by steam-geared turbines which gave a power output of 200,000

8th December 1938. Launching the aircraft carrier „Graf Zeppelin". *(Tadeusz Skwiot)*

Junkers Ju 87C-1, WNr. 0569, GD+FB, test flown in April 1941. Arrestor hook is clearly visible by the tailwheel. *(Via Marian Krzyżan)*

shp, enough to propel her to 34 knots. Initially it was planned to equip the "Graf Zeppelin" with biplanes only, but in 1937 the decision was made to adapt the most modern machines in the Luftwaffe's inventory for carrier-borne service: the ship was to carry a complement of 13 Ju 87 Stuka dive-bombers and 10 Messerschmitt Bf 109 fighters. The only biplane carried was to be the multi-role Fieseler Fi 167 (20 aircraft). In September 1939, at the outbreak of World War 2, the "Graf Zeppelin" was still under construction. On 12th July 1940, when she was 90% completed, it was

Closer look at the folding wing mechanism of the carrier-borne Ju 87C-1. *(Via Marian Krzyżan)*

Messerschmitt Bf 109 T – THE LUFTWAFFE'S NAVAL FIGHTER

The hull of "Graf Zeppelin" after the launching ceremony in December 1938. *(Author)*

Messerschmitt Bf 109 T – THE LUFTWAFFE'S NAVAL FIGHTER

Bf 109 B V-17a coded TK+HM during a test catapult launch. *(Author)*

decided to move the carrier to Gotenhafen (presently Gdynia, Poland) to await the end of the war – which at that time was thought to be near.

However, the fortunes of war proved to be unpredictable: on 16th March 1942 the Oberkommando der Marine (OKM) ordered construction work on the ship to be resumed in order to prepare her for a move back to the Kiel shipyards. In fact, the carrier did not arrive there until 6th December 1942. At this time a project to re-build four ships into auxiliary aircraft carriers was investigated, but the idea was eventually dropped. The defeat at Stalingrad, Hitler's personal aversion to big surface ships and a change at the head of the Kriegsmarine caused a further delay in the construction of the ship, only one month after it was resumed. On 20th April 1943 "Graf Zeppelin" was towed to Stettin (presently Szczecin, Poland), where it remained until the war's end. On the evening of 24th April 1945 the ship's turbines, power generators, lifts and other crucial elements were demolished with explosive charges by German combat engineers. As a result of the Potsdam conference, which settled the division of war booty among the victors, the badly damaged and unfinished "Graf Zeppelin" was taken over by the Soviet Union. The new owners turned the barely floating hulk into a practice target for bombs and torpedoes. On 18th August 1947 "Graf Zeppelin" was hit in the bow by a torpedo fired from the destroyer "Slawniy" and sank.

Prototypes

Design work on Germany's first carrier-borne fighter started at the Messerschmitt plant during the winter of 1937/38. In February 1938 the prototype Messerschmitt Bf 109 V17 (W.Nr. 1776, D-IYMS), based on a Bf 109 C powered by Jumo 210 D engine, was ready for tests. The aircraft was fitted with a tailhook and landing gear wheel fairings designed to prevent the undercarriage fouling the arrestor cables. The machine was test-flown at Haunstetten airfield, and in May 1938 it was passed to an experimental station (E-Stelle) at Travemünde. In July 1938 the aircraft was badly damaged in a take-off accident. After repairs flight tests were resumed. On 16th September 1939 it was coded TK+HK[7].

The other aircraft used to test the Messerschmitt 109's capabilities as a maritime fighter was a Bf 109 B (W.Nr. 301, registered as D-IKAC) delivered to the Augsburg plant on 25th March 1938. It was similarly equipped with an arrestor hook and undercarriage fairings. Shortly afterwards it was transferred to E-Stelle Travemünde, where its civil registration was replaced by TK+HM code. In January 1939 the first test landings with the tailhook were carried out. They showed that the wheel fairings, which were intended to prevent the landing gear from getting entangled with arrestor wires, were redundant. It also transpired that the undercarriage was too rig-

Landing gear wheel fairings designed to prevent the undercarriage fouling the arrestor cables. *(Nowarra)*

id, which caused the aircraft to bounce and hop over the arrestor wires. Out of 31 trials carried out in February 1939 the hook missed the cables on 15 occasions. Hence, on 17th February 1939 new landing gear struts with modified shock absorbers were delivered from the Luftwaffe Test Station at Rechlin. This aircraft was also used in experimental launches from a K5 steam-powered catapult. The first four launches were performed between 18th April and 6th May 1940. The catapult accelerated the Bf 109 to 140 kph, while the pilot experienced gravity forces up to 2.4 g.

In late March 1938 a system of arrestor cables, produced by the DEMAG company, was installed at Travemünde airbase. It was first tested between March and May 1938. On 28th May 1938 an alternative system, delivered by the Atlas-Werke company from Bremen, was also tested. Further test-

Early version of arrestor hook, mounted ahead of tailwheel, in Bf 109 V-17. *(Nowarra)*

„Graf Zeppelin" moored at a wharf. *(Tadeusz Skwiot)*

ing of the modified DEMAG system went on from September to December 1938. Eventually, the DEMAG system was chosen. It comprised stretchable arresting cables, blocked by an electrical device in a preset position that was dependant on the weight of the aircraft, and a mechanical braking device. At 2.8 g and 128 kph the landing run of the Messerschmitt 109 was 26 meters. The arrestor hook mounted under the rear fuselage was 70 cm long and could be lowered by means of an actuating rod. At first the hook proved troublesome for it had a tendency to bounce off the ground and smash against the lower fuselage, damaging it. In order to prevent this, the hook was fitted with a thick rubber bumper.

In August 1938 at Augsburg, Flugkapitän Hermann Wurster test-flew a Messerschmitt Bf 109 E-0 (W.Nr. 1781, WL-IECY) powered by a Daimler-Benz DB 600 G-2 engine. The aircraft was fitted with a tailhook and a new cockpit heating system. In May the aircraft was passed to the E-Stelle at Travemünde, where its civil registration was changed to Stammkennzeichen code TK+HL. The tests with arrestor wires demonstrated that the aircraft had difficulty maintaining its directional stability when landing, so the standard 3.10 m diameter three-bladed VDM propeller was replaced by a smaller one of 2.90 m diameter. A smaller-diameter propeller also meant that the tips were less likely to accidentally chop into the ship's deck!

In order to improve the aircraft's stability, a new wing of increased span (11.08 m) was designed (the Bf 109 E's standard wing measured 9.90 m). The new wings were fitted with special spoilers mounted on the upper surfaces (*Auftriebzerstörer* – literally: lift destroyers), which made landings easier by preventing the wheels from bouncing. In June 1939 the long-span wings were coupled to the Bf 109 V15 (W.Nr. 1773, D-IPHR), which was based on the C-1 version. Since it had previously been used as a prototype for the E version, it was powered by a DB 601 A engine. The Bf 109 V15 was also fitted with an arrestor hook. In the period between July and September 1939 it was test-flown by Hermann Wurster and Fritz Wendel. In January 1940 it received the Stammkennzeichen CE+BF.

On 18th July 1939, E-Stelle Travemünde received a Bf 109 E-0 (W.Nr. 1783, GH+NT), delivered from Augsburg. Fitted with a tailhook, it was used to test landings with arresting cables. Messerschmitt Bf 109 E-3, W.Nr. 1946, D-IGPY (later GH+NU), which made its maiden flight on 16th December 1938 at Augsburg with Fritz Wendel at the controls, was passed to Travemünde at the turn of July and August 1939. In July 1940 the machine was returned to Augsburg, where it was equipped with a new propeller. The Me P6 Bremspropeller ('braking propellor') had an electric motor to regulate the blades' angle of incidence. Although this modification shortened landing runs to 100 meters, the forces generated by the sudden deceleration of the aircraft made a straight landing run virtually impossible. Hence, the device was useless for carrier operations. Another

Another Bf 109 T prototype, Messerschmitt Bf 109 E-0, W.Nr. 1781, W+IECY fitted with a modified arrestor hook. (*Nowarra*)

Close-up of the arrestor hook in Bf 109 E-0, W.Nr. 1781. *(Nowarra)*

problem arising from this solution was that the electric motor used to rotate the blades consumed a great deal of power, which in turn made it necessary to install a more efficient alternator.

After the initial phase of tests, the Messerschmitt design team undertook construction of the Bf 109 T prototype. The suffix "T" denoted carrier (*Träger*)[8]. Luftwaffe pilots nicknamed it 'Toni'. The prototype of the Messerschmitt Bf 109's new version was a modified airframe based on a Bf 109 E-1 (W.Nr. 6153, CK+NC) powered by DB 601 A engine, produced at the Fieseler plant in Kassel. In March the aircraft flew from Kassel to Augsburg, where it was test-flown by Fritz Wendel and Hermann Wurster. In July 1940 the machine was already at E-Stelle Travemünde. It is known that on 6th August 1940 Anton Riediger made two test landings with an arrestor hook. The aircraft was tested until 3rd December 1943.

Serial production

Serial-produced machines were to be built in two variants: the T-1 for carrier service, and the land-based T-2, produced without a tailhook. The new aircraft were mentioned in the Luftwaffe's production plans for the first time in early 1939, when 60 DB 601-powered Bf 109 E-3s were earmarked for conversion to the carrier-borne fighter version, referred to as the Bf 109 Tr. In April 1939 the Lieferplan 11 delivery schedule included 60 Bf 109 Ts (notably, built as such, not conversions from Es). In August 1939 the Lieferplan 13 increased their number to 120. In September 1939 as many as 155 were planned to be built, and in October of the same year even 170. However, in 1940 this number was reduced to 70.

The first serial-production Messerschmitt Bf 109 T, W.Nr. 7728, was manufactured in late January 1941. The first test flights revealed wing vibrations, which delayed further production. The second machine was not completed until early March 1941, and by the end of the month only four more had been assembled. In April 1941 production finally reached the expected output of 25 aircraft per month.

The first Bf 109 T to be lost was W.Nr. 7733, RB+OF. On 3rd April 1941 at 16:02 hrs the machine took off from Haunstetten factory airstrip, with experienced test pilot Fritz Wendel at the controls. It was actually his 5019th flight. He was to test a recent modification – strengthened wingtips. It was suspected that the wingtips were the source of the vibration at high speeds, possibly because their rear section had been modified to house additional lights for nighttime landings. Wendel was briefed to take the aircraft into a dive and check on the new wing construction. The first dive, performed from an altitude of 6000 meters, caused no problems, but during the second dive the aircraft accelerated to 800 kph, and at 3500 meters first the wings, then the entire airframe began to vibrate. Wendel throttled back and unbuckled his seat belts – at the very moment one of the wings broke off and the aircraft went into a tumbling spiral, out of control. The centrifugal force lifted the pilot off his seat and pressed his back against the canopy roof. Seconds later, the other wing ripped away and the canopy tore loose. Wendel, thrown clear, spread his arms and legs wide to stabilize his descent, and pulled the ripcord.

The Messerschmitt design team learned from the accident and duly rejected the thickened wingtip housing the landing lights. A modified aircraft was test-flown by Karl Baur on 30th May 1941. Plunging into a dive, at 3200 meters and at an air temperature of -4°C, he registered a speed of 760 kph. No vibration was detected.

The Messerschmitt Bf 109 T was based on the Bf 109 E-7 airframe. The basic difference was the former's new, 11.08 m long wings, as opposed to 9.90 m on the Bf 109 E-7. The ailerons were lengthened and fitted with an additional hinge. Unlike the Bf 109 E, which featured trim tabs located relatively close to the wingtips, on the Bf 109 T the trim tabs were much closer to the fuselage. The leading edge slats were correspondingly longer, and the upper wings were equipped with retractable spoilers (although on series production machines the mechanism which operated them was deactivated). The aircraft's powerplant was the 1175 hp Daimler-Benz DB 601 N liquid-cooled, in-line engine. It required C3 type 95-octane fuel instead of 87-octane B3, the type more commonly in use in the Luftwaffe. A certain number of aircraft were equipped with the GM-1 boost installation. This system added nitrous oxide to the intake charge to compensate for the reduced oxygen available at high altitude and thereby increased engine power output. The nitrous oxide was stored in four bottles located inside the fuselage aft of the cockpit. Some machines which used the GM-1 installation were also fitted with an additional, nine-liter oil tank, mounted in the port forward part of the fuselage. The increased oil supply was necessary because the boosted engine worked at higher temperatures and consumed more oil. The GM-1 installation was not added to the Bf 109 T until 1942.

The Messerschmitt Bf 109 T was equipped with a Telefunken FuG VII radio set, which worked at frequencies from 2.50 to 3.75 MHz. Its range for contact with the ground was 50 km; this extended to 65 km for communication with another aircraft. The radio system included the FuG 25 IFF ("Identification Friend/Foe") device.

Messerschmitt Bf 109 E-0, W.N r. 1783, coded GH+NT fitted with arrestor hook inspected by Ernst Udet at Travemünde; August 1940. *(Nowarra)*

Fuselage segments of Bf 109 E/T prior to assembling. *(Author)*

Onboard armament consisted of two MG 17 cowl-mounted machine guns with an ammunition supply of 1000 rounds per barrel, which amounted to 55 seconds of sustained fire. Each wing housed an MG FF cannon with 60 rounds per barrel, or an eight-second burst. The Bf 109 T used a standard Revi C/12 reflector gunsight. A dozen or so aircraft were also fitted with an ETC rack for carrying a 300-liter auxiliary drop tank. A total of 70 aircraft of the T version were manufactured. When construction work on the "Graf Zeppelin" was ultimately discontinued, 63 Bf 109 Ts were issued to the Luftwaffe's front-line units.

Hitler's order of August 1941 had demanded that the carrier should be commissioned by 1st October 1942, and so the Kriegsmarine requested that the Luftwaffe should return the Bf 109 Ts. This process began in December 1941, and from April to October 1942 as many as 48 Bf 109 T-2s were rebuilt to T-1 configuration. They were stored at the Kriegsmarine's base in Pillau awaiting completion of the "Graf Zeppelin". However, on 5th April 1943, the Kriegsmarine handed the machines stored at Pillau back to the Luftwaffe in recognition of the ultimate abandonment of the German aircraft carrier project. They were again rebuilt to T-2 standard, which involved removing their maritime equipment before they were delivered to operational Luftwaffe units.

Royal Navy test pilot, Capt. Eric Brown, provided a very interesting opinion on the performance of the Bf 109 T. He had the opportunity to fly nearly all types of captured Luftwaffe aircraft, during and shortly after WW2:

"Take-off – Due to the increased wingspan the Me 109 T would very likely have had no problems lifting off from the 860 ft[9] long deck of the 'Graf Zeppelin' carrier, provided that the wind speed at deck level was at least 30 knots. This view is supported by the assessment of Bf 109 T operations in 1941 by I./JG 77 at Trondheim, Norway. On take-off torque forces pulled the aircraft to the left, away from the carrier deck superstructure, should the pilot take no action to counter it.

Port half of the rear fuselage during assembling process. *(Author)*

Fuselage interior of Bf 109E/T with visible formers and longerons strengthening the construction. *(Author)*

Landing – Putting the Me 109 T back onto the carrier deck would have been quite an achievement, for the forward visibility from the cockpit of a Me 109 E (the predecessor of the 'Toni') was disastrous, and its lateral stability, owing to the uneven action of its slats, was exceptionally poor. On landing approach the Bf 109 E had a tendency to hover for too long in the air. It may be presumed, however, that the purpose-built spoilers mounted on top of the Me 109 T wings would have enabled it to safely touch down on the carrier deck. As the engine rpm decreased, the aircraft immediately became nose-heavy, which forced its pilot to strongly pull on the control column to avoid bouncing off the deck. The Bf 109 undercarriage was infamous for its weak construction, a very undesirable feature for a carrier-borne aircraft that operates under increased gravity forces.

Conclusions – It is my opinion that the Bf 109 T-1 would have been barely suitable for carrier operations. It would have been plagued by the same problems of poor visibility and weak landing gear that haunted the early Seafires[10]. All in all, in my opinion landing a Bf 109 T-1 on a carrier would have been downright dangerous".[11]

One of first serial-production Messerschmitt Bf 109 Ts, W.Nr. 7733, coded RB+OF. *(Author)*

Capt. Brown's comments require some clarification. It was intended that the Bf 109 T-1 would be launched by means of a catapult, not simply take off in the conventional manner; furthermore, the aircraft's handling on landings was much improved in comparison to the E version. The long deck of the "Graf Zeppelin" gave enough room for a smooth landing, unlike the shorter decks of British aircraft carriers, which were the main cause of Seafire crashes. There was not a single accident during nearly 500 test landings carried out with arrestor cables at Travemünde. Also, the forward visibility from a Bf 109 T's cockpit was slightly better than that from a Seafire, as the latter's cowl was even longer.

Wreckage of Bf 109 T, W.Nr. 7733, RB+OF, which crashed on 3rd April 1941. *(Nowarra)*

Operational service

The first 24 Bf 109 T-2 machines arrived in Norway on 1st June 1941, a further 11 on 9th June, followed by 28 more between 12th June and 2nd July 1941. They were assigned to I./JG 77 (47 aircraft) and Jagdgruppe Drontheim (16). Within I./JG 77, commanded by Hptm. Walter Grommes (the Gruppen Stab was stationed at Stavanger-Sola) the Bf 109 T-2s were split among 2./JG 77 (under Oblt. Joachim von Wehren, at Lister), 3./JG 77 (Oblt. Franz Menzel, at Herdla), and 13./JG 77 (Lt. Gerhard Senoner, at Stavanger-Sola). Moreover, a squadron-strong unit known under the designation 4.(Eins.)/JGr. Drontheim, led by Hptm. Joachim Seegert, received a dozen Bf 109 T-2s for immediate operations, plus four reserve aircraft. Seegert's Einsatzstaffel was based at Trondheim-Vaernes, only occasionally making use of an airfield at Oerlandet.

On 15th June 1941, at 13:19 hrs, two machines of 2./JG 77, flown by Lt. Rudolf Glöckner and Lt. Franz Wienhusen, took off from Sola airfield. They were tasked with intercepting a Blenheim, which at 13:25 hrs had unsuccessfully bombed a small Norwegian steamboat. Two minutes after scrambling, the two Messerschmitts attacked the bomber over the sea, some 30 km south of Stavanger. Lt. Glöckner immediately opened fire, setting the British machine aflame. Sgt. Leonard Dowse, the pilot of the Blenheim Mk IV of No 114 Sqn RAF, managed to ditch the bomber. Dowse and his gunner, Sgt. Frank Duffield, were rescued, but the navigator, P/O Charles Starkey, had been shot dead by a burst from the Bf 109s while the Blenheim was still in the air. This victory made Lt. Glöckner the first Luftwaffe pilot to score a 'kill' at the controls of a Bf 109 T-2. A few hours later, at 18:45 hrs, over Egersund, Lt. Hans-Dieter Hartwein of 3./JG 77 knocked down another Blenheim, coded "N", of No 235 Sqn RAF.

On 19th June 1941, at 14:35 hrs, four Bf 109 T-2s took off from Sola on a training flight. At about 15:00 hrs the pilots began shooting at a practice target anchored near Liester. Suddenly, the engine of Bf 109 T-2, W.Nr. 7749, marked

The pilot of Bf 109 T, W.Nr. 7733, RB+OF during its last flight was Fritz Wendel. Here he's seen in the cockpit of Me 209 V1, in company of Willy Messerschmitt (left). *(Author)*

"White 11", flown by Lt. Eckehard Meissel, caught fire. The pilot jettisoned the canopy and bailed out. However, he was only 100 meters above the sea surface and his parachute failed to fully deploy in time to save his life. He was the first fatality among Bf 109 T-2 pilots. Over the next couple of days several minor landing mishaps confirmed the opinion that the Bf 109 T-2 was not an easy aircraft to land and demanded an experienced pilot to fly it.

Another fatal accident occurred at Herdla airfield in the evening of 24th June 1941. At 21:50 hrs, during an alarm scramble, the Bf 109 T-2 W.Nr. 7756, flown by Lt. Rudolf Leow of 3./JG 77 nosed over at the end of the runway and burst into flames. Fähnrich Leow had been promoted by his Staffelkapitän, Oblt. Büchel, to the rank of Leutnant only a few hours earlier. A small celebration party at the officer's mess had just begun when the order to scramble was given.

On Wednesday 2nd July 1941 at 16:10 hrs two Bf 109 T-2s of 13./JG 77 were scrambled from Sola. W.Nr. 7744, RB+QB was flown by Uffz. August Scheimann, W.Nr. 7764, RB+OQ, by Uffz. Kurt Döpfer. When the two Messerschmitts flew out to the sea, they suddenly disappeared from radar monitors. A search operation, which involved aircraft from the air sea rescue service, was undertaken – but in vain. A week later the body of Uffz. Döpfer was found washed up on the beach. A mid-air collision was the most probable cause of this accident. On that day weather conditions were particularly difficult because of a low fog bank over the sea.

On 4th July 1941, at the very late hour of 23:30 hrs, 40 km south of Bergen, Ofw. Gerhard Hornig of 3./JG 77 intercepted and shot down a Blenheim coded RT*X (s/n V6368) of No 114 Sqn RAF piloted by Sgt N. W. Cook. Hornig later served with 5./JG 5 and scored a total 12 aerial victories, before he was killed over Schönwalde on 19th November 1944 in a flying accident at the controls of a Bf 109 G-14.

On 5th July 1941 at 10:15 hrs two Blenheims of No 235 Sqn RAF took off from Sumburgh on a patrol. In the vicinity of Bergen one of them, coded LA*O (s/n N3524) and flown by P/O G. Botham, was shot down off the Norwegian coast by a Bf 109 T. The victor was Lt. Hans Tetzner flying from Königsberg.

On 7th July 1941 Lt. Franz Wienhusen of 3./JG 77 chalked up his first victory; near Vestland he brought down a Blenheim (s/n Z7424) of No 139 Sqn RAF flown by Sgt. Causen. Lt. Franz Wien-

Oblt. Franz Menzel, Staffelkapitän 3./JG 77, and later the re-designated 14./JG 77, during a visit at Lister airfield in summer 1941. Note Bf 109 T-2 in the background. *(Hammel)*

The first Messerschmitt Bf 109 T-2 victory was claimed by Lt. Rudolf Glöckner. From left to right are: Lt. Franz Wienhusen, gunner of shot-down Blenheim, Sgt. Frank Duffield, Lt. Rudolf Glöckner, Blenheim's pilot, Sgt Leonard Dowse and Staffelkapitän 13./JG 77, Lt. Gerd Senoner. (*Author*)

husen was a Kiel native; in 1934 he volunteered for the Kriegsmarine, and a year later applied for a transfer to the Luftwaffe. In August 1940 he obtained his pilot's license at Flugzeugführerschule A/B 118 Stettin-Altdamm. He received fighter training at 2./Jagdfliegerschule 4 in Fürth, which he left on 28th February 1941. In 1942, with the rank of Oberleutnant, he assumed command of II./JG 5. He was killed in action over western Germany while with IV./JG 4, on 3rd December 1944. At that time his victory tally stood at 12.

Another 12 days passed before on 19th July 1941 pilots of I./JG 77 scored another victory. At about 18:20 hrs, off Kopervik, the freighter "Selje" was attacked by a single Lockheed Hudson. Moments later the assailant was tracked down by a Bf 109 T cruising nearby; the victor was again Lt. Hans Tetzner. His quarry, coded NR*W (s/n AM533) of No 220 Sqn RAF, was flown by F/O Russell, who perished along with his crew. For his second success Lt. Hans Tetzner was presented with the Iron Cross I Class. Two weeks later he was transferred to northern Norway, where he served with II./JG 5. In mid-1944 his Gruppe was incorporated into the Reich's defense system to help counter the ever intensifying raids by American four-engined bombers. He was killed in action on 19th July 1944 over Holzkirchen and buried at Preußisch Holland (Pasłęk). At the time of his death his tally stood at 20 victories; he was posthumously promoted to the rank of Hauptmann.

On Thursday 24th July 1941 the Luftwaffe lost its first Bf 109 T in combat. On that day three Beauforts of No 42 Sqn RAF on an anti-shipping mission ventured over southern Norway. The crew of AW*W (s/n L9939) flown by Sgt. Morrison spotted and bombed a small Norwegian vessel "Vestkyst I" of only 370 GRT. One of the bombs punctured the upper deck and went all the way through her hull, tearing a sizable hole in the ship's keel. Although the bomb didn't go off, it caused such extensive damage that at 03:46 hrs the ship sank in a position south of Kristiansand. Her crew safely boarded some rescue boats and reached the shore. Then the British aircraft strafed Ryvingen Fyr, with results unknown. Shortly after 04:00 hrs two Bf 109 Ts of 2./JG 77 approached. The Rottenführer (element leader) was Lt. Werner Minz, and his wingman was Uffz. Werner Schramm. The Beaufort's gunner, Sgt. Robert McNab, waited for the Messerschmitt flying on the left to close to 160 meters before he loosed off a burst of 120 rounds. The German fighter was hit and nosed into the sea. The other Bf 109 broke off the attack and flew away. Uffz. Schramm landed at 04:48 hrs and reported the scrap with the enemy. He stated that Lt. Minz had engaged a British bomber, but at that moment Schramm had lost sight of his leader. He claimed

The primary opponents of Messerschmitt Bf 109 T-2s in summer 1941 were British Bristol Blenheim Mk. IV bombers. Seen here is Mk IVL serial-numbered V5382. *(Author)*

to have chased the bomber until it disappeared into a bank of fog. An immediate search operation was launched using a Heinkel 59 floatplane, but the body of Lt. Minz was never found. The lost machine was Bf 109 T-2, W.Nr. 7777, marked "Black 8" (with red outline).[12] Operations in July 1941 brought the Bf 109 T pilots four victories for the loss of one aircraft in combat and four more in accidents. There were three fatalities among the pilots.

On 1st August 1941, Oblt. Hans-Christian Schäfer was appointed the new Staffelkapitän of 2./JG 77. Schäfer had served earlier with JG 26, and in spring 1940 took over 5./JG 27. On 19th May 1940 he was shot down by a French Morane MS-406 fighter and was made a PoW. He was released from captivity after the fall of France in late June 1940. Schäfer was not very well liked by his subordinates; one of them, Kurt Hammel, described him as a *Dummer Hund* after the war.

On 5th August 1941 at 13:31 hrs Lt. Franz Wienhusen successfully engaged and shot down one of two Hudsons, which had bombed the patrol vessel "Murmel" (VP 5509) in Bjornafjord. The British machine, Hudson Mk V, NR*R (s/n AM625) belonged to No 220 Sqn RAF and was piloted by Sgt E. Ashworth. The entire crew was posted as missing. In the early afternoon of 6th August 1941 Sola radio station plotted a single bomber flying at 1,300 meters. As the aircraft made landfall, the contact was lost. At 14:03 hrs an alarm Rotte of 13./JG 77 was scrambled. The leader was Lt. Gerd Senoner, with Lt. Alfred Jakobi on his wing. At 14:30 hrs they spotted the lone Hudson and Lt. Senoner engaged from the rear quarter, firing a short burst. Then Lt. Jakobi took his turn. Meanwhile, the leading machine flown by Lt. Senoner made a wide orbit and swooped down for a second pass. The British bomber weaved violently in a series of evasive maneuvers, seeking refuge in patchy clouds, while the gunner fought off the attacks with his machine gun. One bullet smashed against the leading Messerschmitt's canopy; Senoner felt a stabbing pain in his eye, where a splinter of Plexiglas lodged itself. He immediately broke off the attack and turned for his home base. Meanwhile, Lt. Jakobi followed the bomber and when it finally emerged from the haven of the clouds, the German nailed the Hudson with a long burst in its starboard engine. Tongues of flame lapped hungrily from the engine, then the landing gear flopped down and finally the Hudson nosed down. Jakobi took no chances and let go one more long burst. As the rounds hit home, the bomber, already doomed by fierce fires enveloping its engines, was torn apart by an internal explosion; only flaming pieces fell into the sea. Lt. Jakobi's

Oblt. Mildner, intelligence officer of I./JG 77, posing by Messerschmitt Bf 109 T-2 of 2./JG 77. With his back turned to the camera is Lt. Robert Müller, a pilot of Gruppenstab I./JG 77. *(Hammel)*

One more snapshot of the same scene, with Oblt. Mildner sitting on the wing. *(Hammel)*

On 7th July 1941 Lt. Franz Wienhusen shot down a Bristol Blenheim of No 139 Sqn RAF. *(Author)*

victim was Hudson Mk V, NR*F (s/n AM583) of No 220 Sqn RAF flown by P/O R. S. Jameson. At the end of 1941 Lt. Jakobi was transferred to 5./JG 5. After he scored his 10th victory, on 9th April 1942 he was shot down and captured by the Russians. He survived the captivity and died in 1978 in Frankfurt am Main.

The following day, 7th August 1941, 24-year old Uffz. Egon Neumann of 13./JG 77 was killed on a training flight. For unknown reasons his Messerschmitt Bf 109 T-2, W.Nr. 7775 plummeted from a height of 500 meters straight into the sea.

On Monday 11th August 1941, coastline observation posts reported an enemy bomber and Lt. Jakobi and Uffz. Heinrich Scharf took off to intercept. Shortly before 13:00 hrs the two Germans located a single machine at 1,000 meters. It was a Blenheim LA*F (s/n P6908) of No 235 Sqn RAF flown by P/O W. Richards. On sighting the interceptors the Blenheim pilot turned north and made a run for his life. The Rotte of Messerschmitts quickly closed in. Lt. Jakobi flamed the bomber's port engine with one burst. To his surprise the Blenheim just flew on and there was no return fire from the rear gunner. It began to descend, streaking thick, dark smoke, then snapped into an unrecoverable spin, crashing 20 km south west of Stavanger. Jakobi, who on that occasion flew a Bf 109 T-2 marked with "White 6", used only 60 machine gun rounds to knock down his opponent.

In the early morning of 18th August 1941, off Stavanger, a Hudson Mk III, NO*N (s/n T9413) of No 320 Sqn RAF flown by F/L Langelaar, fell to the guns of Uffz. Heinrich Scharf of 13./JG 77, with the loss of the entire British crew.

On Saturday 30th August 1941 at 14:58 hrs two Bf 109 T-2s of 2./JG 77 were scrambled from Lister. Barely 18-years-old, Lt. Kurt Hammel led the pair with Fw. Alfred Flamm on his wing. Their task was to locate and destroy three Hudsons reported near the coast. Hammel reminisced:

"Hapless Lockheed Hudsons: the poor fellows who had flown them to Norway stood no chance against us. However, since they often flew low and only in bad weather, they were not easy to spot. These were chance encounters. They approached low over the water, with the cloud base at 150 meters and the moment we tried to attack them they pulled up and disappeared into the murk.

[…] I was a young Leutnant then. At about 15:00 hrs Fw. Flamm and I were scrambled. Immediately after our take-off I noticed some flare signals (red puffs of smoke) fired by our 8.8 cm Flak guns. Most of our alarm scrambles occurred in response to reports from anti-aircraft posts, which had spotted enemy aircraft. Our radiolocation stations were rarely able to detect aircraft flying so low. The Flak battery that had alerted us was located near the lighthouse at Lister.

We were flying on a westerly course straight towards the sea. The red marker puffs could be seen to our right. Straining my eyes, I caught sight of two dots heading north. I called them out to Fw. Flamm over the R/T, but he didn't alter his course accordingly. I banked to the right and rammed the throttle forward, heading at full bore towards the enemy aircraft. They were flying at about 30 meters above the sea; their crews had apparently not noticed me. I had no problem overtaking them – my 'Toni' was much faster. As a matter of fact, I was closing in at high speed. I maintained my altitude at barely ten meters and continued to fly beneath them undetected. When I had cut the distance to some 200-250 meters, I opened fire at the machine flying to the left. It was definitely from too far out, but I had little experience then. I was lucky though, for the port engine of the Hudson instantly burst into flames. Its nose dropped and then it slashed into the water at a flat angle and disappeared. I engaged the other machine. After a short burst I could see the results of my fire. The aircraft began to leave a trail of thickening smoke. However, as I sped past and over it, the rear gunner hit me. As I turned toward the coast, I noticed Fw. Flamm – who had finally arrived at the scene – launch an attack against the damaged Hudson. The British machine landed in the sea, hitting the surface of the water at a flat angle. Moments before ditching, the pilot pulled the nose up, but the aircraft nevertheless broke apart upon impact. I found out later that a Do 24[13] had picked up the crew. Two seriously injured crewmembers were transported to an aid station at Stavanger. Both aircraft were crewed by Dutchmen".[14]

Kurt Hammel survived the war and scored 23 victories, although he himself was shot down three times. The two downed Hudsons belonged to No 320 Sqn RAF. On that day the squadron lost one more machine, brought down by Lt. Ehrler of 2./JG 77.

In August 1941 the Bf 109 T-2 pilots claimed a total of seven enemy aircraft shot down for the loss of one pilot killed, one injured, two of their own machines destroyed and seven more damaged.

On 1st September 1941, Uffz. Johannes Ranwig of Jagdgruppe Drontheim, flying a Bf 109 T-2 marked "White 10", shot down a photo-reconnaissance Spitfire (s/n X4500). The British pilot, F/O C.C. Blair, was killed.

The following day British Beaufort torpedo aircraft of Nos 22 and 42 Sqns RAF set upon a small convoy off Stavanger, sinking the "Oslebshausen", a 4,989 GRT freighter loaded with iron ore. A somewhat belated intervention by Messerschmitt Bf 109 T-2s brought about two victory claims by Oblt. Schäfer and Lt. Senoner. In fact, the British lost only one Beaufort, the machine coded OA*W (s/n AW218) of No 22 Sqn RAF, piloted by Sgt. McTavish.

Early September 1941 saw the combat debut of a new aircraft, which over the following years was to dominate the daytime skies over Germany. It was the four-engined Boeing B-17 Flying Fortress. In mid-1941, it was issued to the RAF as the Boeing Fortress Mk I (B-17C). The first machines of this type, delivered in April 1941, equipped No 90 Sqn RAF stationed at Polebrook.

On Saturday 6th September 1941, four Fortresses of No 90 Sqn were tasked with bombing the German heavy cruiser "Admiral Scheer" reported at Oslo harbor. The raid was fruitless, for all the bombs missed. The Bf 109 Ts that were scrambled to intercept failed to make contact with the new adversary. Two days later four Fortresses of No 90 Sqn once again raided southern Norway. This

Messerschmitt Bf 109 T-2, "White 3" of 4.(Eins.)/JGr. Drontheim at plank-paved airfield of Trondheim-Vaernes, summer 1941. *(via Barbas)*

time the Germans were luckier. Lt. Alfred Jakobi and Lt. Wolfgang Steinicke of 13./JG 77 were the first to engage. At the debriefing Lt. Jakobi reported as follows:

"On 8th September 1941 I was part of an Alarm-Rotte flying Bf 109 Ts. After take-off we were vectored by the 'Bee'[15] to assembly area No 1. Before I reached the assigned area, I saw two contrails above and ahead of me, made by aircraft flying from west to east. I was flying from north to south. I turned towards the contrails, gaining altitude. As the enemy aircraft made landfall, the contrails disappeared. I maintained my previous course. Corrected by the 'Bee', at a height of 8600 meters (which was also my altitude) I saw a black dot against the hazy horizon. After 12 minutes of flying at full throttle, without further climbing, I found myself some 400 meters away from a four-engined bomber. I recognized it as a Boeing. I took note of its defensive armament, probably 2 cm twin-mounted cannons, judging from their bright muzzle flashes as they opened fire at me. At the same time I was fired upon from two machine guns mounted in a dorsal turret, which was located at a point one-third of the fuselage length from the nose.

At a distance of 400 meters I fired my two machine guns, and as I began to close the gap, I let go with my entire onboard armament. My wingman, Lt. Steinicke, who was flying slightly lower, fired at the same time. When the bomber skidded to one side so as to give its waist gunner a field of fire, I scored cannon hits on the rear starboard section of the fuselage. As I drew closer, I saw a large hole in the bomber's rear fuselage and flames enveloping its tailfin. I saw no ventral gun positions. My bursts caused the port outboard engine to streak smoke. I broke away to line up for a second firing pass. At the same time the enemy banked to the left and I instinctively followed him. Then I noticed that the bomber had jettisoned six to eight bombs (which looked like 500 kg types). I was also fired upon during my second attack, but I managed to score hits on the port wing, tearing off large bits. The bomber began to shed pieces and smoke poured out of its cockpit. It spiralled down, followed closely by my wingman. I called a warning to him over the R/T: 'Watch out, it could blow up at any moment!'

The enemy aircraft fell into a steep dive and exploded some 2000 meters below me. Temporarily blinded by the flash, I was unable to observe the falling debris nor locate the point of the crash."[16]

The other B-17 fell prey to a Bf 109 T-2 of 2./JG 77 flown by Uffz. Karl-Heinz Woite. It was his first victory. Woite perished in a flying accident on 22nd July 1943 and was buried at Stargard. The British registered the loss of two Fortress Mk Is: WP*N s/n AN533 flown by Sqn/Ldr A. Mathieson, and WP*D, s/n AN525 flown by F/O D.A.A. Romans. A third Fortress, WP*O s/n AN535 flown by Sgt M. Wood, was severely damaged but managed to return to base where it made a wheels-up landing. Damaged beyond repair, it was written off.

On Wednesday 10th September 1941 three torpedo Beauforts of No 22 Sqn RAF harassed a small

On 19th July 1941 Lt. Hans Tetzner shot down a Lockheed Hudson of No 220 Sqn RAF. *(Author)*

Messerschmitt Bf 109 T-2 of 2./JG 77 having its DB 601 N engine checked; Lister airfield, summer 1941. *(Hammel)*

convoy protected by two Kriegsmarine trawlers, of which one was hit and sunk. Again the Messerschmitt cover was late. Only several minutes after the attack did a Rotte of Bf 109 T-2s of 3./JG 77 intercept the retreating British machines. Lt. Wulf-Dietrich Widowitz laid claim to one Beaufort destroyed. Nevertheless, the British machine (coded OA*J s/n X8930, flown by Sgt. Jennings) limped back to base and crashed on landing. At a later date Lt. Widowitz was posted to JG 5 and tallied a total of 36 victories. His comrades held him in high esteem, for he often flew a Fieseler Storch deep behind enemy lines to pick up downed German airmen. He was killed in July 1943 aboard a Gotha Go 145 (DB+DF) liaison aircraft.

In September 1941 the Bf 109 T-2 pilots chalked up six RAF machines for the loss of two of their own (both wrecked in accidents) and a further three damaged.

On 4th October 1941 at 15:12 hrs Ofw. Gerhard Hornig shot down a Hudson of No 220 Sqn RAF (NR*O, s/n V9066) piloted by P/O V.G. Collins. Another October victor was Oblt. Hans-Christian Schäfer, who knocked down a Beaufort of No 42 Sqn RAF (AW*N, s/n N1163) on the 14th, flown by W/O J.E. Woodward. Two days later, on 16th October 1941, at 17:08 hrs an Alarm-Rotte of Bf 109 T-2s, flown by Lt. Kurt Hammel and his wingman Uffz. Fritz Schütze, took off from Lister. Hammel recalled:

"I spotted an enemy aircraft, which I recognized as a Bristol Beaufort. It was flying at 150 meters, just below some clouds. The overcast was 6/8 at 150 meters, and 8/8 at 300. I attacked from below, firing a long burst. The Beaufort turned west, running for the clouds. Since the cloud deck was thin and wispy, I could follow it without losing visual contact. I closed in but refrained from shooting. I noticed that the rear gunner was knocked out of action; the barrels of his twin-mounted machine guns were motionless and pointing skywards. I overtook the Beaufort and waggled my wings, hoping to force it to turn inland, but in vain. When I engaged it, the British began to perform violent evasive manoeuvres. Still, I hit it with a few bursts, whereupon the

On 24th July 1941 Sgt Robert McNab, a rear gunner in Bristol Beaufort of No 42 Sqn RAF, shot down Bf 109 T-2, W.Nr. 7777 marked with "Black 8" (red-outlined). The Messerschmitt's pilot, Lt. Werner Minz of 2./JG 77, was killed. *(Author)*

Beaufort snapped onto its back and hurtled into the sea at a steep angle".[17]

On Sunday 19th October 1941, Lt. Wulf-Dietrich Widowitz downed a Hudson Mk V of No 220 Sqn RAF (NR*W, s/n AM724), flown by F/S W.H.R. Smith. October ended with a tally of four RAF aircraft for the Bf 109 T pilots against the loss of one Messerschmitt wrecked on landing and two more damaged in similar circumstances.

Atrocious weather conditions throughout November 1941 seriously hampered the operational activity of both sides in the coastal areas of southern Norway. The Bf 109 T pilots scored only a single victory during that period. On 23rd November, Lt. Wolfgang Steinicke bounced and quickly dispatched a Hudson Mk V of No 608 Sqn RAF (UL*T, s/n AM715) flown by F/S R.H. MacMillan. Steinicke later served with III./JG 5 and in October 1943 was transferred to 12./JG 2 stationed in France. He was killed in combat with a formation of American four-engined bombers on 2nd March 1944.

In November 1941, I./JG 77's own losses amounted to two aircraft destroyed, two damaged and one pilot killed. The fatal loss was Uffz. Ernst Steinborn of 3./JG 77 who flew a Bf 109 T-2, W.Nr. 7795, coded "Yellow 3".

On Tuesday 2nd December 1941, Lt. Edgar Habermann of 3./JG 77 bagged a Hudson Mk III, (NO*O, s/n V9036) of No 320 Sqn RAF over the sea. Its pilot, F/L Jan Dolmann was a Dutchman, as were all the other crewmembers. Two days later, on 4th December, Uffz. Rudolf Fenten claimed to have shot down another Lockheed Hudson off Stavanger. In fact, it was one of the first reconnaissance Mosquitos to be seen over Norway.

Flown by Sqd/Ldr A.L. Taylor, it was a Mosquito PR I (T*LY, s/n W4055, which carried the name "Benedictine" on the fuselage). German pilots stationed in Norway had not been briefed about the possibility of encountering this new type from the RAF inventory, so the misidentification is understandable. Besides, the shapes of the fuselage and wings made the two types appear somewhat similar at a distance. Rudolf Fenten, the pilot who downed the Mosquito, had enlisted with the Luftwaffe in early 1939. After his training at Jagdfliegerschule 5 he was posted to I./JG 77, and in early 1942 to JG 5. On 19th February 1943, his Bf 109 G-2 was shot down by Russian anti-aircraft artillery. Fenten was captured and spent the rest of the war in a POW camp.

The Saturday of 13th December 1941, was to be an unlucky one for 3./JG 77. At 14:20 hrs Uffz. Günter Streb took off in a Bf 109 T-1 (W.Nr. 7761) from Herdla. After eight minutes of flight the aircraft's engine began to cut out and throw oil. Streb attempted an emergency landing, but his machine bounced heavily off the ground and skidded over a high cliff nearby, crashing down into the sea below. Streb was killed.

Ten days later, on 23rd December 1941, the Luftwaffe High Command issued the following order to Luftflotte 5 (5th Air Fleet):

"By order of the Reichsmarschall, all serviceable aircraft designed to serve as carrier-borne fighters are to be handed over to the Kriegsmarine. All Bf 109 T-2s are to be withdrawn from active service and converted to T-1 standard". At that time, Luftflotte 5 had about 30 Bf 109 T-2s on strength, with five Bf 109 T-1s in storage at Erding.[18]

In a new role over the North Sea

During the first few months of 1942, a total of 46 aircraft were converted from T-2 to T-1 standard at the Fieseler plant in Kassel. However, by that time a new variant of Messerschmitt's fighter, the Bf 109 G, was entering production. The Luftwaffe High Command decided that it would prefer to develop the then-latest G variant into a carrier-borne fighter (eventually, this role was to be assigned to the Messerschmitt Me 409 design). Hence, the pool of available Bf 109 T-1s was relegated to training duties. The 46 converted Bf 109 T-1s were transferred to an airfield at Pilau, where they were joined by the five machines previously stored at Erding.

In early 1943, Hitler decided against completing any of the Kriegsmarine's large surface ships still under construction. This meant that the German Navy no longer had any use for the Bf 109 T-1s, so they were transferred back to the Luftwaffe. Their tailhooks were dismantled (although the catapult fittings were retained) and on 30th April 1943, the first 11 machines were issued to the Jagdstaffel Helgoland. A further 13 were delivered to NJG 101, a night-fighter training unit. At least one Bf 109 T-1 was also operated by a Wilde Sau[19] outfit, Stab der III./JG 300. In the latter part of 1943 the T-1s of NJG 101 were passed to Jagdstaffel Helgoland. This semi-autonomous fighter squadron had a checkered career of considerable successes and heavy losses.

The island of Helgoland, standing like a lone sentry off the German coast along the North Sea, formed an important part of the Reich's Air Defense system. It was located directly beneath the flight path of an approach route often used by USAAF bombers as they headed for major German seaports like Hamburg, Lübeck and Kiel. As early as 1940, a plan to construct an airfield on the island for Luftwaffe interceptors was conceived. The construction work commenced in June 1941, and by August 1942 the runways were ready. Shortly afterwards it transpired that the main runway was too short, and by April 1943 it had been lengthened to measure a total of 795 meters. The strip was made of concrete, and was thinly coated with asphalt.

Besides the airfield, the island also housed radar stations and Flak batteries. The main task of the Helgoland garrison was to harass the ever-growing formations of four-engined Boeing B-17 Flying Fortresses. By spring 1943 the American bombers were still flying unescorted, so it was decided to risk the ageing and outperformed Messerschmitt Bf 109 Ts against them.

The first document that certifies the decision to move Messerschmitt Bf 109 Ts to Helgoland is dated to 17th March 1943. It was a written order by Gen. Maj. Adolf Galland, the Inspector General of Fighters, given to Maj. Heinrich Brustellin. On 7th April 1943 Jagdstaffel Helgoland was officially commissioned (previously the shortened name of Jasta Helgoland was used). The unit was operationally subordinated to II./JG 11 commanded by Obst. Adolf Dickfeld.

Lt. Gerd Senoner, who was injured in action on 6th August 1941. (*Author*)

Ground crew checking on Bf 109 T-2, W.Nr. 7778, "White 8" at Trondheim-Vaernes, summer 1941. *(via Barbas)*

The same aircraft having its engine warmed up prior to take-off. Note Fug 25 antenna under fuselage. *(via Barbas)*

A few days before, on the afternoon of 31st March 1943, an unusual recruitment of flying personnel for Jasta Helgoland took place. Each candidate from a group of pilots gathered at Jever airbase was to perform five landings in a Bf 109 T-1 "Green 1". The five pilots who made the shortest landing runs were assigned to the new unit. These were: Uffz. Ewald Herhold, Uffz. Karl-Heinz Kutzera, Uffz. Oskar Menz, Uffz. Otto Turowski and Fw. Erich Carius. Hptm. Egon Falkensamer, who was expected to assume command of Jasta Helgoland, lost out in the competition to Oblt. Hermannem Hintzen. The latter was 32 years old, and had previously (from January 1941) served with I./JG 1. In November 1942 he was appointed Staffelkapitän of 3./JG 1. As a side note, in civilian life he had been a confectioner by profession.

On 17th April 1943 the pilots of Jagdstaffel Helgoland made their combat debut. On that day 115 Flying Fortresses of the 91st, 303rd, 305th and 306th Bomb Groups struck off for the Focke-Wulf plant at Bremen. Despite staunch opposition in the air and heavy anti-aircraft fire around the target area, the American bombers broke through. The 265 tons of bombs they dropped wreaked havoc on the ground. Nearly half of the plant's buildings were destroyed, along with 30 brand-new Focke-Wulf Fw 190 A fighters. At about 13:00 hrs the returning raiders flew out to sea, with some 30 Luftwaffe fighters still buzzing around them. At 13:15 hrs the order to scramble was sent out to Jasta Helgoland. Four Bf 109 T-1s took to the air, climbing at full throttle to an altitude of 8000 meters. One of the four pilots who participated in this action was Uffz. Ewald Herhold:

"After climbing through a cloudbank Carius and I spotted two bombers, which apparently had dropped out of their Pulk defensive formation. Both Boeings were flying relatively low and we tagged onto them. Carius was slightly ahead of me. We didn't expect much success, but as we opened fire, the bomber on the left was hit and one of its engines burst into flames. Since it was flying in my line of fire, I was the victor. Carius reported our position over the radio so that the bomber crew, provided they managed to bail out, could be rescued. Then Carius called me saying: 'I have to turn back – with the fuel I have left, I'll get only as far as Borkum'. So we were already too far out.

The other bomber, which escaped our bursts, banked to the right and disappeared in the haze. Meanwhile the burning bomber shed its starboard wing. Its entire crew of ten bailed out. I passed over the spot of the crash to let them know that I would direct a rescue party to pick them up. The Americans waved back at me with a signal flag. However, when I made one more pass over the spot, I noticed that the wreck of the bomber had already submerged and that only one man was still afloat in a dinghy. The remaining crewmembers had disappeared; they must have been dragged under the water by the whirlpool created by the sinking aircraft. I circled the spot five times but all I could see down below were floating oxygen bottles and debris. Since my fuel was getting low, I had to turn back".[20]

Lt. Kurt Hammel in the cockpit of Messerschmitt Bf 109 T-2 at Lister airfield. The aircraft in the background is marked with "Red 3". *(Hammel)*

Messerschmitt Bf 109 T-2, W.Nr. 6363, "White 10" of JGr. Drontheim, flown by Uffz. Johannes Ranwig. Note Fug 25 antenna under fuselage. *(Nowarra)*

Jasta Helgoland's own losses were limited to one aircraft, Bf 109 T-1, W.Nr. 7762, shot down by the B-17 gunners. Its pilot, Uffz. Oskar Menz took to his parachute and an hour later he was 'fished out' by a Luftwaffe rescue service floatplane. The Americans lost a total of 16 Flying Fortresses on that day, which amounted to 14% of the deployed force. The Germans claimed 19 bombers destroyed and two HSS[21], for the loss of two of their own machines (the American gunners claimed 63 German fighters destroyed, 15 probably destroyed and 15 damaged). The heavy losses deterred the USAAF from making further forays against the Reich for four weeks.

On 15th May 1943, American bombers targeted shipyards at Emden and Wilhelmshaven. At 10:21 hrs, Bf 109 T-1s of Jasta Helgoland took off to challenge them. The Messerschmitts turned on a 30° heading, climbing as ordered up to 8000 meters. Barely four minutes had passed before the German pilots noticed tight formations of four-engined bombers, which they engaged at 10:35 hrs. Despite 40 minutes of continuous attacks not a single bomber fell prey to the Messerschmitts.

On 1st September 1941 Uffz. Johannes Ranwig flew this aircraft when he shot down a reconnaissance Spitfire s/n X4500 piloted by F/O C.C. Blair (who was killed). *(Nowarra)*

It was apparent that the Bf 109 T's armament, which consisted of two 20 mm cannons and two 7.92 mm machine guns, was hardly sufficient to bring down a mighty Fortress. Small machine gun bullets were not capable of damaging the vital mechanisms and installations of the B-17s, nor could the outdated wing-mounted MG FF/M cannons deliver a big enough punch. Due to their relatively poor muzzle velocity, the rounds they fired carried little kinetic energy. On average, it took 20 rounds from this type of cannon to knock down a four-engined bomber.

Meanwhile, shortly before 11:00 hrs Helgoland itself became a target for 80 bombers, which unloaded their bombs from an altitude of 7000 meters. No fewer than 70 bombs impacted on the island, of which 15 hit the airfield. Ten civilians were killed and 30 injured.

On Wednesday 19th May 1943, a formation of 103 B-17s targeted Kiel, whilst a further 55 went after the Flensburg shipyards. On their return leg, over the North Sea, the bombers were bounced by a couple of Jagdstaffel Helgoland's Bf 109 T-1's. Oblt. Hintzen and Uffz. Kutzera claimed a B-17 apiece. One of the Messerschmitts coded "Green 4", flown by Uffz. Herhold, was slightly damaged (a stray .50 cal round hit its port wing flap). The Germans claimed ten B-17s; the Americans' actual losses were six. The Luftwaffe's losses amounted to two machines from III./JG 54. Interestingly, the bomber gunners claimed 71 fighters destroyed and 35 more damaged!

Two days later, on 21st May 1943, the U.S. 8th Army Air Force again struck off for targets along the German North Sea coast. After bombing Wilhelmshaven and Emden, at about 12:33 hrs the returning Fortresses appeared over Helgoland. The interceptors of Jasta Helgoland were already in the air and two minutes later they attacked. Again, despite numerous passes at the bombers, the under-gunned Bf 109 T-1s were unable to inflict telling damage. Fw. Erich Carius, who flew the machine marked "Green 1", scored the only victory. On that day the Luftwaffe fighter pilots claimed 17 bombers for the loss of three aircraft and two pilots. The USAAF's actual losses amounted to 14 B-17s; the gunners claimed 89 fighters shot down and 23 damaged. For the first time, bomber crew reports mentioned 'long-winged' Messerschmitts, which were reputedly "very fast, had a wingspan estimated at 40 feet and presumably a radiator under the nose".

On 26th May 1943 command of the unit was taken over by Oblt. Hermann Behrend, a native of East Prussia. At that time, Jasta Helgoland could field 17 Bf 109 T-1s, of which 12 were combat ready. Deteriorating weather forced a three-week pause in operations. It was not until the afternoon of 11th June 1943 that the Americans staged another raid against Wilhelmshaven and Cuxhaven. The Alarm-Schwarm of Jasta Helgoland scrambled at 17:32 hrs. Four minutes later, Leitstelle Jever[22] reported an enemy formation passing over Helgoland at 7000 meters. Between 17:50 and 18:00 hrs the Bf 109 T-1s made several unsuccessful attacks. One Messerschmitt broke off the fight with a damaged engine and returned to base.

On Sunday 13th June 1943 fair weather encouraged the U.S. Eighth Army Air Force to strike at the U-Boot shipyards at Kiel and Bremen. When pilots of Jasta Helgoland were ordered to take off at 09:00 hrs, the American bombers were only 50 km away from the island. Two minutes later, the

Lt. Günther Eggebrecht in the cockpit of Bf 109 T-2 "White 2", summer 1941 (Author)

On 8th September 1941 No 90 Sqn RAF lost two Fortress Mk Is intercepted by Bf 109 T-2 s. *(Author)*

commander, Oblt. Behrend, received a report on the enemy's position. At 09:13 hrs the first Rotte – the Staffelkapitän himself and Uffz. Herhold – made visual contact with the bombers bound for Kiel. The two Germans gunned their engines and gave chase, which carried them to the outskirts of Neumünster. Uffz. Herhold recalled:

"When we were ordered to take off, the commander came up to Carius and me and said, 'Carius, you'll fly with Kutzera, and Herhold will join me'. I replied, 'Herr Oberleutnant, I would like to point out that here, in the Reich's defense, we fly in a different manner than in Russia. Here enemy bombers approach at the altitude of 10,000 meters and this is where we have to fight them. Our tactics are simple, we have to strike from above, otherwise our attack doesn't make much sense'.

Obviously the commander, being my superior, ignored my remarks and said nothing. He ordered me to cover him, so that he could have a go at the bombers. That sounded fine in theory, but did it work that way?

We warned the commander not to open fire from too far out. We had to get as close as possible because we knew that the enemy gunners only became aware of our presence once we had opened up on the bombers and then they instantly returned fire. I also realized that in my Katschmarek position I was going to attract the lion's share of enemy bullets.

Of course, our Staffelkapitän opened up too early and before I knew it, we were charging straight into the middle of a group of 20-30 bombers. I was promptly hit and lost sight of my leader. The Staffelkapitän passed through the enemy formation unscathed and returned to Helgoland. Meanwhile, I turned around and made a head-on pass at a bomber that was flying on the left flank of the penultimate Pulk. I lined him up properly in my sights and most of my rounds tore into the bomber's cockpit; still, he maintained his position in formation. Again, I manoeuvred into a good firing position and immediately saw the results of my burst. The Boeing Fortress II spun down and disintegrated. Burning pieces fell to the ground at 09:25 hrs in the 95876 grid position.

My own aircraft was hit directly in the engine, and my radio set and tail were shot through. I was at 7000 meters. During a headlong attack things happened very fast: establishing one's own position, manoeuvring, firing, and breaking off the attack… Since my engine still worked, I began to gain altitude, but as I attempted to level off, the first flames appeared. The bombers were fading away into the distance; I still had time to get my bearings. I could see both the North Sea and the Baltic Sea. This meant that if I were forced to bail out, at least I would jump over land. Flames began to sear into the cockpit, so I jettisoned the canopy. In a Messerschmitt this was done manually, by pulling a lever. By doing this I hoped to improve my situation, but it only got worse. Dense smoke and oily soot belched into my cockpit. I thought: 'I've had it'. I was pinned down in my seat and the aircraft was in a steep dive. Somehow I managed to undo the straps and with a sudden jolt I was thrown clear. Beforehand, I had made sure that my parachute harness was properly tightened. I tumbled past the fuselage and suddenly was stopped in mid-air when my

Messerschmitt Bf 109 T-2, W.Nr. 7745 "Red 1" of 2./JG 77, damaged on landing at Lister on 8th September 1941. *(Hammel)*

leg got hooked on the tailfin. I fell free but the fin broke my right leg. In my right calf I also had a bullet wound, which I hadn't noticed earlier. A piece of metal that was embedded in my knee remains there to the present day.

I was falling freely until I reached the cloud deck at some 4000 meters; then, with my left hand, I pulled the ripcord. The parachutes we used in those times were a far cry from the modern designs, for we were falling at six meters per second. Suspended under the canopy and all alone, I finally had time to gather my wits. Descending towards the ground, I saw a city in the distance. All that time I was drifting in a fairly strong wind. Was it Kiel, or somewhere else? It turned out to be Boostedt near Neumünster. It was the first parachute jump of my life. I wanted to bend my knees and roll over as per instructions, but in the end I hit the slope of a railway embankment. Thank God the canopy immediately deflated and collapsed onto the ground, while I slid down the embankment and landed in a meadow. I was lucky because a row of tall poplars ran along the embankment and I could easily have hung myself on a treetop. After the sirens had sounded to mark the end of the air raid alarm

Before an aircraft could be taken to the base workshop for maintenance, fuel had to be pumped out of the fuselage tank. *(Hammel)*

in Neumünster, I saw the first Heimatwehr[23] vehicles, which had been dispatched to find me. Two men approached me and shouted from a distance, 'Are you German or American?' I called back, 'Heil Hitler!'

'Everybody calls Heil Hitler, Americans too!' they shouted at me.

Since my face was completely black and I was dressed in leather overalls, they couldn't make up their minds as to my nationality. In those times Americans were falling from the skies too. I yelled back, 'Hell, I'm a German!' They checked my papers and finally relaxed.

We weren't carrying our soldier's paybooks around, only red-colored ID cards. There was nothing in them but a photo portrait and home address, with no data on our military service, unit assignment or anything like that. That was classified information. About ten minutes later, a car arrived to carry me to an aid station, where a medical professor operated on me. Although it was the Pentecost holiday, the professor and his wife took personal care of me.

Before the day was out, I had the opportunity to make a phone call to my base at Helgoland in order to inform them that I was still alive and that I had been operated on in Neumünster hospital. It had all happened so fast: 09:00 hrs scramble, 09:30 hrs air combat, 10:00 hrs in hospital".[24]

Before he left hospital, Uffz. Herhold received the Iron Cross Second Class for his second victory. He also received the 'Bronze Wound Badge' (*Verwundetenabzeichen in Bronze*).[25]

On that day the bombers' return fire also hit Bf 109 T-2, W.Nr. 7769, flown by Fw. Erich Carius. He managed to crash-land on Föhr island, his mount suffering 40% damage. At about 11:00 hrs the returning American 'heavies' were attacked by a Rotte of Bf 109 Ts and Oblt. Hintzen shot one down. The outcome of the air battle of 13th June 1944 was a definite victory for the Luftwaffe, which claimed 32 bombers shot down for the loss of only four fighters with three more damaged in crash landings. The Americans' actual losses were 27 B-17s that failed to return and a further 54 with battle damage. Of the 76 machines that raided Kiel, 22 went down, which was nearly 30% of the deployed force. The loss of so many aircraft – along with 250 airmen – must have been quite a shock for the American Air Force High Command. The Americans suspended further operations over Northern Germany until fighters fitted with long-range fuel tanks became available for escort duties.

On Sunday 4th July 1943, Oblt. Behrend relinquished command of Jasta Helgoland and returned to I./JG 11. He was succeeded by Lt. Erich Hondt of 6./JG 11. Before he enlisted with the Luftwaffe, Hondt had been an art history student. He received his pilot's rating in 1942 and started his combat career with JG 53 in North Africa. Later, he was posted to I./JG 1 at Jever. His parents lived in Vienna, and in his first letter home, Hondt wrote:

"Jasta Helgoland is part of our Geschwader and operates from a coastline sandbank. On this

Messerschmitt Bf 109 T-2, "Red 9" of 2./JG 77 on a patrol off the coast of Norway, autumn 1941. *(Hammel)*

Messerschmitt Bf 109 T-2 damaged on landing. This machine was piloted by Gruppenadjutant I./JG 77, Lt. Robert Müller. *(Author)*

Another shot of the same machine, showing the supplementary armored windscreen. *(Author)*

marvelous island, besides an inexhaustible store of liquor, one can also find a kind of nervous tension experienced by all the 'islanders'. Through this appointment Major Mader (Geschwaderkommodore of JG 11 – author's note) has made me the youngest Staffelkapitän in the Geschwader. This is my first command post; I didn't expect to be tasked with something like this so soon. Work, work, and more work! I reached the island onboard a Fw 58 'Weihe'. We fly Bf 109 Ts here, which are relatively slow and under-armed. For two hours every day we perform training flights – which are exceptionally difficult. After additional sports exercises and other activities we are so tired we forget about girls and hit the sack."[26]

German fighter pilots took advantage of this brief period of inactivity, not only training but also resting and enjoying their seaside summer, as recalled by Uffz. Erich Ulmschneider: "The summer of 1943 was a charming time for us. I used to go swimming in the North Sea quite a lot. In the evenings we would get onboard a boat to cruise over to 'Aunt Lotty'. Fw. Erich Carius had got himself a license to pilot motorboats for this precise purpose; he was our steersman. At 'Aunt Lotty' we had a grand selection of excellent liquors. On Sunday afternoons our girlfriends could visit us for a cup of coffee (the real, grained coffee!) at our 'dune airfield'. Those were great times spent at Helgoland with the island's fighter squadron!"[27]

On Saturday 17th July 1943 an aerial armada of 332 four-engined bombers from 1st and 4th Bomb Wings took off from their bases in England and set course for Germany. At 08:48 hrs five Bf 109 Ts scrambled from Helgoland to challenge them. They were flown by: Lt. Hondt, Fw. Carius, Uffz. Ulmschneider, Uffz. Menz and Uffz. Turowski.

A few minutes after take-off they came across the bombers. At the debriefing Lt. Hondt reported the following:

"I was flying as Staffelführer. After we made contact with the enemy, we flew parallel with the bomber formation for another five to ten minutes; then, at 09:10 hrs, we turned around for a head-on attack. I fired at the bomber flying third from the right flank, roughly in the center of the massive formation which was staggered up and down. I saw hits on the bomber's fuselage and port inboard engine. During the pass my left aileron got shot off. Struggling with the controls, I attacked another Pulk flying behind the first, lower and to the left. After that I returned to base. According to eye-witnesses the machine I had fired at dropped out of formation and headed down, trailing a thin streak of smoke, approximately north-west of Helgoland".[28]

The Fortress hit by Hondt – a B-17F (s/n 42-3219) named "Dear Mom" and commanded by 2/Lt. Robert P. Powledge – fell into the sea north of Helgoland. This was confirmed by Uffz. Otto Turowski, who had shot down another Fortress at 09:24 hrs, a B-17F (s/n 42-29872) named "Snow Ball" piloted by Lt. William E. Peters. Lt. Hondt's wingman in this action was Uffz. Erich Ulmschneider:

"The Americans returning from Wilhelmshaven were flying along the northern route, passing

Bf 109 T-2 W.Nr. 6363. On 29th November 1941 Uffz. Erich Kersten was killed while flying this aircraft. *(Nowarra)*

Messerschmitt Bf 109 T-2, coded "Green 3" of Jagdstaffel Helgoland; Helgoland, spring 1943.
The aircraft in RLM 74 Graugrün, RLM 75 Grauviolett and RLM 76 Lichtblau finish.

Messerschmitt Bf 109 T-2, „zielona 3" z Jagdstaffel Helgoland, lotnisko Helgoland, wiosna 1943 roku.
Samolot pomalowany kolorami RLM 74 Graugrün, RLM 75 Grauviolett i RLM 76 Lichtblau.

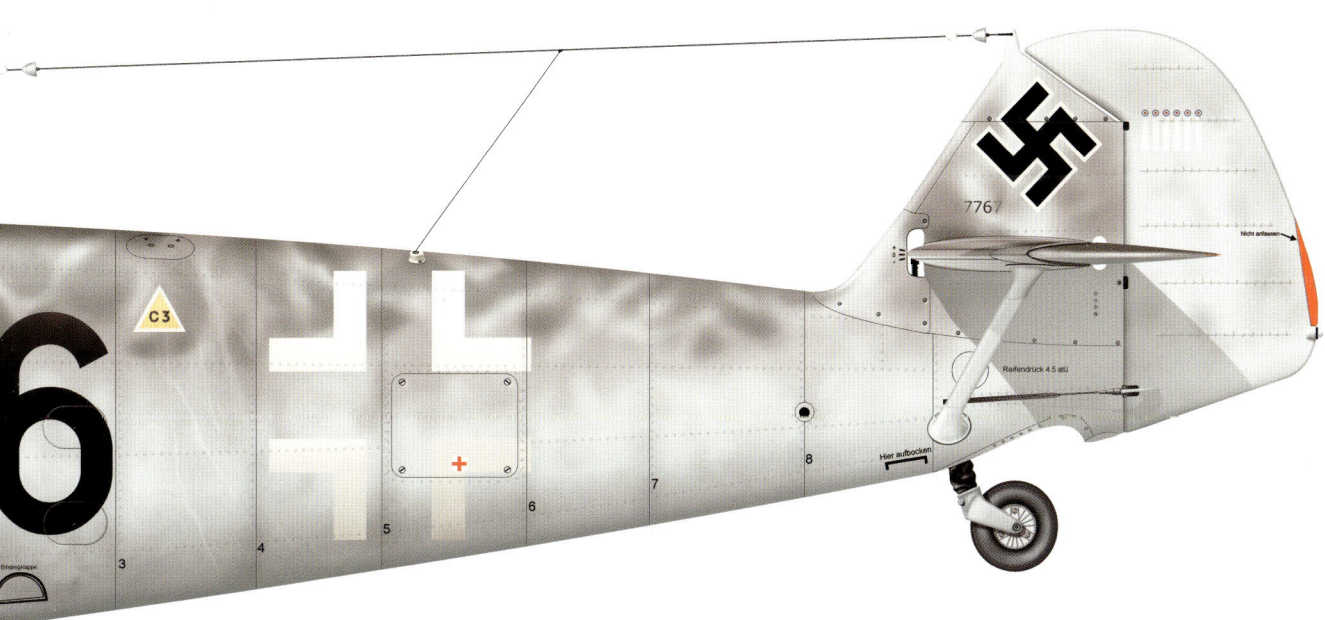

Messerschmitt Bf 109 T-2, W.Nr. 7767, coded "Black 6", flown by Oblt. Herbert Christmann, Staffelkapitän 11./JG 11.
Lister, Norway, winter 1944.

Messerschmitt Bf 109 T-2, W.Nr. 7767, „czarna 6", pilot: Oblt. Herbert Christmann, dowódca 11./JG 11.
Lotnisko Lister, Norwegia, zima 1944 roku.

MAGAZINES BY KAGERO

www.kagero.pl

Do nabycia:
kioski RUCH, punkty sprzedaży Empik i Kolporter, supermarkety...
oraz w sprzedaży wysyłkowej – www.kagero.pl, tel. 081 749 20 20

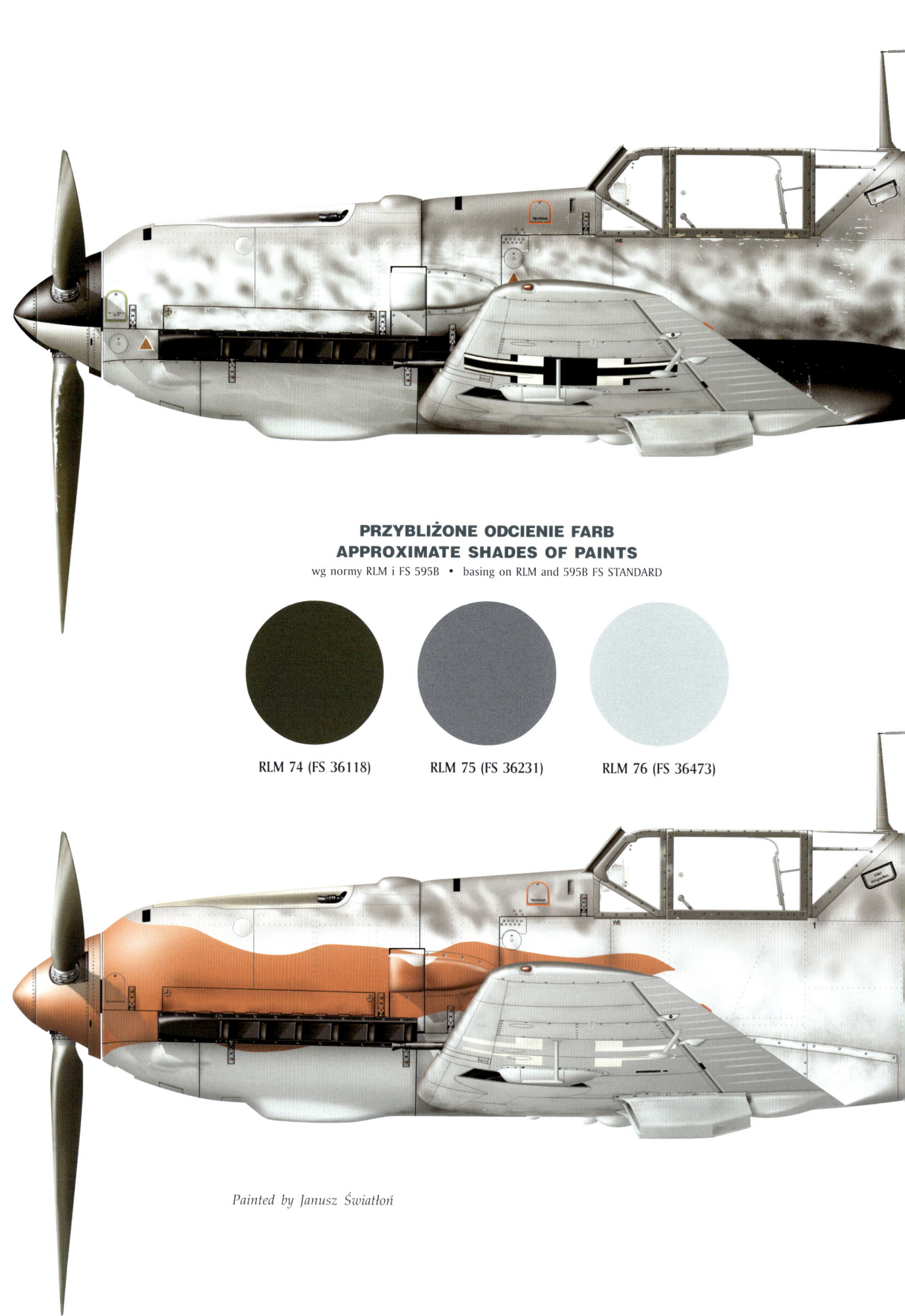

**PRZYBLIŻONE ODCIENIE FARB
APPROXIMATE SHADES OF PAINTS**

wg normy RLM i FS 595B • basing on RLM and 595B FS STANDARD

RLM 74 (FS 36118)   RLM 75 (FS 36231)   RLM 76 (FS 36473)

Painted by Janusz Światłoń

In 1943 this Messerschmitt Bf 109 T served as a trainer in NJG 101, a night fighter training outfit stationed at Manching airfield. White letter N visible on the engine cowling identifies DB 601 N engine. *(F. J. Marshall, Messerschmitt Bf 109T. Die Jäger der ›Graf Zeppelin‹)*

by Helgoland. As we climbed, we saw a formation of 20-25 B-17s at 6000 meters. We turned on a converging course, whereupon we went past the enemy formation, keeping the distance at some 1500 meters. We left them behind in order to turn around and attack from the front. It took a lot of time since we were doing 420 kph. As soon as we outdistanced the bombers by three kilometers, we veered around to port and headed back. Lt. Hondt was charging flat out into a Pulk of Viermots. Fw. Carius and three other machines lagged behind us. Hence, initially only the two of us slashed through about 30 Boeings, and all their gunners zeroed in on us. I was possessed by some kind of 'hunter's fever'. At a distance of 1000 meters I caught one of the B-17s in my sight. I opened fire with my machine guns. As I was about to press the cannons' trigger, something slammed into my aircraft. I was violently pushed back into my seat and I couldn't see anything. Before commencing my attack I had raised my anti-shrapnel goggles in order to have a better view. A round from an American machine gun had punctured my armor-glass windshield, throwing a hail of splinters into my face and eyes. I expected to collide head-on with the Viermot any second, but nothing happened. From the corner of my teary eye I noticed tracers coming at me from behind. But I was safe – I had flashed past the bomber without colliding with it! When the tears had stopped welling up in my eye, I was able to look around. There were no Boeings, nor even any of my squadron mates to be seen. 'Turn south,' I said to myself, 'sooner or later, you'll make landfall'. My aircraft calmly droned on, and I slowly regained some confidence".[29]

Uffz. Ulmschneider landed safely at Wangerooge where his injuries were taken care of, before he was returned to his home base.

Uffz. Oskar Menz was far less lucky. His Bf 109 T-1, W.Nr. 7753, "Green 4" was shot down by cross-fire from the bombers. He managed to bail out and fell into the sea. Menz had never learned to swim and lived in constant fear that one day he might drown because of a faulty inflatable life jacket. For this reason he was the only pilot in the Staffel to use an old life jacket, which used cork blocks for buoyancy. In a cruel twist of fate, after a few hours of floating in the sea his cork jacket soaked through and pulled the hapless pilot to the bottom before he could be rescued.

On Sunday 18th July 1943 a new pilot, Uffz. Rudolf Dölling of 6./JG 11, was assigned to Jasta Helgoland. In a letter to his parents he gave an interesting account of a day in the life of a Jasta Helgoland pilot:

"We woke up at 03:30, but didn't get up before 06:00. Then we moved to our airfield, which was some 400 meters from our living quarters. There we again rested until 08:10, when we had breakfast. Then I wrote letters until noon. Afterwards we had a luxurious dinner: asparagus, potatoes, stew and the like, everything deliciously cooked. There are nine of us and we have our own cooking lady, who obviously can adjust to our individual tastes. Never before have I eaten so well and so lavishly. Is there really a war going on out there? In the afternoon I slept for two hours and had a game of chess. At 18:30 we had a supper, equally sumptuous. Later I played the accordion for a while. At 20:00 I was already in a movie theater. This is the best part of my stay here: every day a movie is shown; every other day they play a new one.

At 22:30 I had a quick swim in the North Sea, my first time ever. You won't believe how utterly surprised I was by the salty taste of the water. I can still taste it in my mouth. But the swim itself was pure pleasure. It's not cold at all. Then I sat down again to write some more letters. That's more or less how my day here has passed. I'm billeted with other pilots in one of our barracks. We live two per room, very comfortably. The rooms are beautifully furnished and steam-heated, with running water available in each room. We have a carpet on the floor and, of course, beds with mattresses. But the biggest luxury for me is a telephone next to my bed. So, I cannot complain really. Every day, except Sundays, a ship cruises between Wilhelmshaven and Cuxhaven. Our mail comes and goes onboard steamers".[30]

The idyllic life on the island came to an abrupt end on Sunday 25th July 1943, when the Americans launched their 'Blitz Week', which was aimed at hitting ten targets in Germany over six consecutive days. On the first day of the operation two groups of bombers struck at Kiel and Hamburg.

At 14:54 hrs, the Bf 109 Ts of Jasta Helgoland took off, but their pilots missed the enemy formation, which had altered course. The German fighters returned to base at 15:27 hrs. The ground crews immediately refuelled them and at 16:08 hrs the Messerschmitts were back in the air. Between 16:16 and 16:20 hrs, in the vicinity of Hamburg, they attacked some B-17s of the 1st Bomb Wing. At 16:55 hrs Lt. Hondt claimed a victory:

"Five of us took off against the Boeings. I bagged one near Hamburg; seven crew members bailed out. The burning wreck cratered into a grain field."[31]

Another Fortress was shot down by Uffz. Turowski at 17:32 hrs. The bomber, already damaged by other fighters or anti-aircraft artillery, was flying at barely 3,500 meters. Finished off with a few bursts, it plunged into the North Sea.

The following day, 26th July 1943, the Americans again targeted the Hamburg shipyards. Another target on that day was a tyre factory in Hannover. Jasta Helgoland fighters took off for the first time at 10:37 hrs, but made no contact with the enemy and half an hour later returned to base.

At 11:23 hrs, after topping up their fuel tanks, the Staffel again took to the air. The Messerschmitts strenuously climbed up to 8,000 meters heading west, then southwest. At 11:40 hrs the bombers were reported 40 km north of Norderney Island, flying at 8,000 meters. Twenty minutes later another report located the enemy formation 50 km north of Borkum, while a second group of bombers was spotted 40 km west of Cuxhaven.

Pilots of Jagdstaffel Helgoland (from left): Uffz. Ewald Herhold, Fw. Erich Carius and Uffz. Oscar Menz *(via Barbas)*

Fw. Erich Carius by a Bf 109 T-2, Heligoland, July 1943. *(via Barbas)*

Two minutes later, over the island of Wangerooge, the interceptors clashed with a group of 36 B-17s. At 11:55 hrs, Uffz. Dölling shot one down; his personal account of the victory was quoted in the opening passages of this book.

Another Flying Fortress fell to the guns of Uffz. Erich Ulmschneider:

"Some time between 11:00 and 12:00 hrs we heard the airfield loudspeaker blurt out the hated word 'Scramble!' They're coming. We had been sitting in our cockpits for a couple of minutes already, at full readiness. Mechanics cranked our Messerschmitts' engines into life. It was a warm summer and the engines caught at once, so we revved them up and began to taxi out. The Alarm-Start, drilled so many times before, went smoothly. We made an obligatory turn to the left before reaching the island's shoreline to avoid the barrage balloons, which protected us from low-level air raids. Then the eleven Bf 109 Ts of the Jasta formed up and turned northeast, towards the Boeings.

After half-an-hour of flight we finally saw them at 7,000 meters. A tense silence fell over our cockpits, only the calm voice of our commander could be heard over the R/T: 'Many Dicke Autos[32] ahead, we're going in!' After a small correction to our course we found ourselves exactly in front of a Pulk of 30 Fortresses. They were looming ever larger. My heart, beating fast, went up to my throat. I felt a curious mixture of fear and 'hunter's fever'. To the right of us, Lt. Hondt had already led the first Schwarm in an attack. The second Schwarm under Fw. Erich Carius (who was my element leader) flew more to the left and to the rear. There was still a gap of some 1,500 meters between the bombers and us. From then on everything happened fast – I flicked on my Revi gunsight and re-charged the guns. Then I lined up a Viermot in my sight. The Fortresses stubbornly pressed on, throwing a furious barrage of machine gun fire at us. At a distance of 1,000 meters I caught one in the glowing crosshairs of my Revi. There was just time to zero in with my machine guns, before hammering the bomber with the two wing cannons. I fired a short burst from my machine guns, and then pressed the cannon trigger – nothing! I ducked under the bombers and banked away, desperately trying to reload, but to no avail. The blasted guns had jammed!

Lt. Erich Hondt, the commander of Jagdstaffel Helgoland.

I turned for Helgoland in a wretched mood, made a lousy landing and taxied to the service area.

The ground crew rushed to mend the malfunction. It was a trivial thing, but it had serious consequences: a spent cartridge had got stuck and made a short circuit; a circuit breaker had triggered and everything stopped working. Away in the distance I could hear the throb of engines and the clamour of gunfire, whereas I was sitting uselessly on the ground! After 20 minutes my Messerschmitt was ready to go. I was ordered to wait in readiness for a signal.

Suddenly, everyone cocked their ears to the drone of engines coming from the northeast. A single aircraft could be seen at 4,000 meters. It was a B-17, a lone straggler limping back to England. It was the American crew's undoing to pass by so close to Helgoland. I sprinted back to my machine faster than ever before, as the mechanics fired up the engine. My 'Me', the last 'Toni' ready for action, lifted off the ground at full bore. I cursed and praised my aircraft: 'You damned sluggish duck, my dear, good 109, get moving, faster, faster!'

When I had cut the distance to 1,000 meters and prepared myself for a pass, I noticed that the enemy bomber was making no attempt to evade or fire back. What was wrong with them? Perhaps there were injured onboard, otherwise they would have noticed me and reacted accordingly. I was closing in; 400-500 meters. I was planning to find my mark with a burst from the machine guns, then to blaze away with all barrels. Wait! This can't be true! I could clearly see dark dots dropping away from the Boeing and the first 'chutes opening. The bomber's commander must have realized the odds against him and given his crew the order to bail out. I sighed with relief, for I was all ready for a real shoot-out. When I had counted eight parachutes and witnessed the Boeing hurtle into the sea, I turned back to Helgoland, overcome with relief and joy in my heart: 'You won't have the fate of these men weighing on your conscience!'

Back at my home base, I twice passed over the airfield waggling my wings, then touched down, this time making a perfect, three-point landing. There was a good reason to celebrate, for all my squadron mates had returned safely with the news of one victory confirmed and another probable. Our Staffelkapitän saw to it that the bomber crew was picked up from the sea as quickly as possible by a rescue service launch. In the evening we went to celebrate our successes of the day at 'Aunt Lotty'."[33]

The Staffelkapitän, Lt. Hondt was forced to break off the attack when eleven-.50-cal rounds fired by the bombers' gunners hit his Messerschmitt. Hondt nursed his damaged fighter back to Helgoland, where he landed safely. Uffz. Dölling shot down a B-17F (s/n 42-30279) named "Black Jacker", flown by 2/Lt. Jack W. Daniel[34]. It crashed near "Alte Mellum", a sandbank in the vicinity of Wangerooge. Three crew members survived: engineer Staff Sergeant Edwin H. Buck, radio operator Sergeant Wayne W. Pringey and the pilot, Second Lieutenant Jack W. Daniel. Another victor was Uffz. Ulmschneider who shot down a B-17F (s/n 42-5895) named "Souse Family", flown by Lt. Theo R. Harris[35]. The American pilot had initially intended to ditch the aircraft, but later changed his mind and ordered the crew to bail out. Those in the front section of the bomber jumped, but the remaining crewmembers had gathered in the radio compartment (the usual place to shelter during an emergency landing) and failed to hear the order. Miraculously, three of them survived the plunge into the sea and were later rescued by a boat from 4. Seenotstaffel. Of the seven airmen who had taken to their parachutes, only three survived: the pilot, the bombardier and the engineer.

On Wednesday 28th July 1943, the pilots of Jasta Helgoland took off at 09:35 hrs for their third

Lt. Hondt in the cockpit of his Bf 109 T. Of note are oval covers of access hatches to GM-1 installation. *(Author)*

combat mission of the day. At 09:58 hrs, northwest of the Dümmer See, they set upon a group of Flying Fortresses of the 4th Bomb Wing, which had targeted the Focke-Wulf plant at Oschersleben. Lt. Erich Hondt led the interceptors:

"On my first pass I shot down a bomber, which made a 180° turn and went down. Then my engine was hit and the canopy oiled over, obscuring my view. I manoeuvred for a second pass, but any success would have been purely down to luck, for I could hardly see outside the cockpit. Thick, black smoke filtered into the cockpit, and the engine began to falter. I had to put down my shot-up crate somewhere. During my emergency landing I chopped down two trees and a telegraph pole. Finally, I came to a halt in a cloud of billowing dust in the middle of a cornfield. When I came to, I had an excruciating headache, and found I was lying on a sofa in a big, rural house. My aircraft had been completely destroyed by a combination of six direct hits and a hard bellylanding. I found out I was near Meppen, by the Dutch border".[36] Interestingly, when the Luftwaffe recovery team arrived at the scene of the crash, they estimated the damage suffered by Hondt's Bf 109 T, W.Nr. 7781, "Green 2" at merely 50%. Lt. Hondt's victim was a B-17 of the 412th Bomb Squadron, 95th Bomb Group (s/n 42-30150), flown by 2/Lt. Fred D. Hodges. It carried the name "Exterminator".

The following day, 29th July 1943, the airfield at Helgoland became a secondary target for 32 American bombers, which due to cloud overcast failed to locate their primary target, the Deutsche Werke plant at Kiel. A total of 117 incendiary bombs (of 250-lb. type) fell onto the island and 80 more into the sea nearby. The impromptu raid did not result in any considerable damage. Three pilots of Jasta Helgoland gave chase to the bombers. Among them was Lt. Hondt:

"An Alarm-Start in the morning. Three of us went after a big group of bombers and finally caught up with them. I veered around, opened fire, and one of my cannons jammed! I made several passes, flashing through a criss-cross of tracers. I saw my rounds find their mark and streaks of smoke trailing behind the damaged bombers, but none of them fell! I was overcome by feelings of fury and despair, and fired again, thinking: 'Have some more from me!'

Then my engine took a hit. In a split second my cockpit was filled with smoke. I conquered the overwhelming urge to bail out and pushed the nose of my machine down into a dive. In the heat of the battle I had ventured too far out to sea

Lt. Hondt, wearing an American army-issue airman leather jacket, posing in company of five young natives of Heligoland, with a Messerschmitt Bf 109 T in the background. *(F. J. Marshall, Messerschmitt Bf 109T. Die Jäger der ›Graf Zeppelin‹)*

and now there was no land to be seen on the horizon. My engine spluttered and belched smoke. Again, I felt like bailing out. I couldn't see a thing. I jettisoned the canopy. In the distance I saw a pall of smoke drifting skyward. Helgoland has been bombed! The mainland was too far anyway, so I bellied in on the cratered runway, a horror to behold! Another aircraft wrecked. Very soon there will be none left to fly!"[37]

Curiously, this time also the Luftwaffe recovery team considered Hondt's aircraft, Bf 109 T, W.Nr. 7746 coded "Green 7", repairable (only 35% damage). The unit, however, lost another Messerschmitt, Bf 109 T, W.Nr. 7769, flown by Uffz. Wilhelm Massoth. Riddled with bullets in a shoot-out with a B-17s' gunners, it was wrecked during an emergency landing at Leck. The injured Uffz. Massoth was hospitalized.

The loss of three aircraft and the intensive operations during the last week of July 1943 temporarily took the starch out of Jasta Helgoland's operations. On 30th and 31st July 1943 not a single aircraft in the unit's inventory was airworthy and the Jasta's pilots had to remain on the ground. In the first half of August 1943 the average number of aircraft serviceable on any one day never exceeded three. On 9th August 1943, Lt. Hondt

Main adversary of Messerschmitt Bf 109 Ts of Jasta Helgoland were B-17Fs, American heavy bombers. Seen here is "Knockout Dropper" of 303rd Bomb Group. *(Author)*

relinquished command of Jasta Helgoland, reverting to the leadership of 2./JG 11 stationed at Husum. He was succeeded by Oblt. Friedrich Bartels, who hitherto had served with JG 52 on the eastern front. Uffz. Ulmschneider wasn't particularly sorry to see his commander leave:

"Hondt came to us only because he suffered from what we called 'Knight's Cross fever'. At Helgoland it was simply too peaceful for him. He was a daredevil who didn't care for his own safety, nor for the safety of the men he flew with".[38]

Erich Hondt was not to gain the award he coveted so much. On 8th October 1943 he was shot down and seriously injured. He spent six months in hospital recovering from extensive burns. He returned to active service only to be shot down and injured several times more. In March 1945, after scoring 16 victories and completing almost 150 operational sorties, he was posted to JV 44 for conversion onto on the Me 262. He survived the war but the numerous injuries he had suffered during his frontline service sapped his health and eventually led to his premature death at the age of 54.

On 2nd September 1943, Jasta Helgoland lost one of its most promising pilots. Uffz. Rudolf Dölling lost control of his Bf 109 T-1 W.Nr. 7772 coded "Green 5" during some low-level aerobatics and plunged into the sea. The following day the wreck was hoisted from the seabed with the pilot's body still trapped inside. Rudolf Dölling, who had enlisted with the Luftwaffe in October 1940, was credited with one Flying Fortress while serving with Jasta Helgoland.

In mid-September 1943 another change of commander took place: Oblt. Friedrich Bartels, was posted to I./JG 11 and replaced by Oblt. Hans-Heinrich König. The latter was born on 23rd July 1921 in Halle. On 1st October 1939 he joined Fliegerausbildungsregiment 12 at Königsberg-Neumark; he held the rank of Fahnenjunker at that time. After training, he was assigned to 5./ZG 76 in February 1941. With this unit he scored his first two victories over the North Sea. At the end of 1941 his Staffel was absorbed into III./NJG 3. In June 1942 he scored two more victories. On the night of 26th June 1942, during an attack on a British bomber, he was severely injured and lost one eye. After three months in hospital he was granted permission to return to flying. Initially, he was an instructor at II./Nachtjagdschule 1. Later he managed to get an operational posting to the day fighter arm.

On Thursday 30th September 1943, a Rotte of Bf 109 Ts scrambled to intercept a solitary enemy reconnaissance aircraft flying along the German North Sea coast. After nearly an hour of fruitless searching the two fighters returned to base. At the end of September 1943 Jasta Helgoland had 16 machines on strength, of which 11 were serviceable.

On 4th October 1943 the U.S. 8th Army Air Force went after targets located in Frankfurt am Main and in the Saarland region. In order to disperse the German defense force, 38 B-24 Liberators of the 44th and 392nd Bomb Groups mounted a decoy raid against targets in northern Germany. Their task was to cross the North Sea and then quickly turn back to England before making landfall. However, the ruse did not work out as planned. After German radars had plotted the American bombers' course, nine Bf 109 Ts of Jasta Helgoland took off from Jever at 09:38 hrs[39]. They were accompanied by fighters of II./JG 11. At 09:45 hrs enemy bombers were reported some 150 km west of Helgoland. At 09:56 hrs the Bf 109 Ts, having climbed up to 7,000 meters, spread out into their combat formation. At 10:09 hrs the German pilots made visual contact with the enemy formation. The ensuing scrap lasted 20 minutes and Oblt. Hans-Heinrich König – the new CO of Jasta Helgoland – shot down a Liberator.

The pilots of Jasta Helgoland failed to record any additional victories in October 1943. Their own losses in that month were: one aircraft (Bf 109 T-1, W.Nr. 7736) wrecked in an emergency landing and two damaged.

By the end of October 1943 the arrival of winter was imminent and the weather worsened. The Staffel was therefore transferred from the island to an airfield at Liester in southern Norway (although some aircraft and flying personnel remained at Helgoland). The runway at Liester was covered with wooden planks, which made it particularly dangerous in rainy and windy conditions.

On 3rd November 1943, the engine of Oblt. König's Bf 109 T (W.Nr. 7734) packed up as he was returning from a patrol. The seasoned veteran safely ditched the aircraft and climbed out of cockpit. His wingman fixed his position and alerted the Kriegsmarine's coastal defense ships. A patrol boat picked up König shortly afterwards.

Over the following few days, the Bf 109 Ts flew a series of uneventful patrols protecting convoys along the Norwegian coast. Finally, on 18th November 1943, around 13:00 hrs, Jasta Helgoland fighters intercepted a formation of 102 B-24 Liberators that were on a mission to bomb an aviation factory at Kjeller in Norway. In the ensuing clash, which went on for a couple of minutes, Uffz. Willi Walbeck, Uffz. Walter Kirchner and Uffz. Ernst Breton claimed one American bomber apiece. However, only moments after scoring his first victory, Uffz. Breton was killed in the cockpit of his Bf 109 T, W.Nr. 7735, coded "Green 24". The aircraft dived into the sea, and the pilot's body was not found until 6th December 1943, when it was washed up on a Swedish beach near Skaftö. Another aircraft of Jasta Helgoland, Bf 109 T, W.Nr. 7745, was extensively damaged during an emergency landing in the Frydsbrömnd area of Denmark.

On 30th November 1943, Jagdstaffel Helgoland was officially re-commissioned as 11./JG 11. Together with 10./JG 11 it formed 'Kommando Skagerrak', led by Hptm. Siegfried Simsch, who also acted as the Staffelkapitän of 10./JG 11.

On 4th December 1943 command of the unit, by this time known as 11./JG 11, passed to Oblt. Herbert Christmann, who had previously served with JGr. 50. Oblt. Hans-Heinrich König, the erstwhile Kapitän of 11. Staffel, took over 3./JG 11. In May 1944, König was promoted to Gruppenkommandeur of I./JG 11. However, before the month was out, König had perished along with his last quarry. On 24th May 1944 a Boeing König had fired at exploded in mid-air, ripping off a wing from his Fw 190. His Focke-Wulf tore into the ground near Kaltenkirchen, with the pilot still in the cockpit. At the time of his death his score stood at 24, including 20 four-engined bombers. On 2nd September 1944 he was posthumously awarded with the Knight's Cross. The Bf 109 T pilots' last encounter with the enemy in 1943 occurred on 23rd December. A Rotte of Messerschmitts scrambled to intercept a reconnaissance Mosquito of No 333 Sqn RAF. However, the intruder outran the pursuers and ducked into the clouds.

On Friday 14th January 1944 a group of 24 Beaufighters of Nos 144 and 404 Sqns RAF attacked two small convoys off the coast of Norway. Seven Bf 109 Ts of 11./JG 11 strove to fight off the assailants. Uffz. Emil Kohl claimed two Beaufighters, and Uffz. Paul Rohe contributed with another claim. Despite the presence of German fighters the British managed to sink two

Uffz. Erich Ullmschneider by his Bf 109 T-1. Note catapult fitting behind the main landing gear wheel strut. *(via Barbas)*

steamers: "Entrerios" (5179 GRT) and "Wittekind" (4029 GRT), and damaged the escorting minelayer "Kiebitz" (VP 5307).

Uffz. Emil Kohl was not to bask in his success for long, for on 20th January 1944 he was killed in a flying accident. The crash was witnessed by Ofw. Georg Weinmann of Stab IV./JG 5:

"I was flying via Oslo to Drondheim-Lade. Besides my Junkers W 34, there was only a Focke-Wulf Fw 58 of the Air Sea Rescue Service at the airfield. Unfortunately, during my brief stay at Kristiansand I witnessed the fatal crash of a Bf 109 T, which resulted in the death of a young pilot. He came in low over the field and zoomed up. Suddenly he stalled and fell off towards the ground. At the last moment he attempted to pull up, but his machine mushed into the ground at quite a steep angle. The pilot was killed on the spot. The engine of the Bf 109 was half buried in the ground, and the fuselage was smashed flat."[40]

In February 1944, inclement weather conditions hampered operations of both the USAAF and the Luftwaffe. Nevertheless, the Americans launched Operation "Argument", better known by its unofficial nickname "Big Week". It was aimed at neutralizing the German aviation industry. On the third day of the operation, 22nd February 1944, the primary target was to be an aircraft plant in the Halberstadt-Bernburg area. Again, the Americans staged a simultaneous, diversionary raid. Some 30 Fortresses of the 92nd, 96th and 305th Bomb Groups separated from the main bomber stream and turned towards Denmark and the Luftwaffe airfield at Aalborg.

At about 14:00 hrs the Bf 109 Ts of 11./JG 11 took off from Lister and were vectored towards Grove. After 50 minutes of flight the Messerschmitts ran into a group of B-17s. The Staffelkapitän, Oblt. Herbert Christmann, was the first to claim a Flying Fortress (at 14:50 hrs), his sixth victory. Six minutes later, Fw. Franz Ritschel notched up his fifth. At 15:00 hrs Uffz. Karl Merbeth laid claim to his first victory, also a B-17. The fourth Fortress fell prey to Uffz. Walter Kirchner (it was his second victory) at 15:05 hrs, at the altitude of 6,000 meters, some 20 km west of Stenbjerg.

2/Lt. James L. Liles of the 326th Bomb Squadron witnessed the demise of the B-17G named "Hot Rock" (s/n 42-97494) of the 325th Bomb Squadron, 92nd Bomb Group:

"I saw a B-17 some 150 meters below us, at one o'clock. It went into a steep dive, and then

Messerschmitt Bf 109 T, W.Nr. 7767, "Black 6" at Lister airfield. The aircraft sported a painting of stylized flame extending from the propeller spinner along fuselage side. *(F. J. Marshall, Messerschmitt Bf 109T. Die Jäger der ›Graf Zeppelin‹)*

One more shot of the same machine, this time photographed during a tuning of its FuG VII radio set. *(F. J. Marshall, Messerschmitt Bf 109T. Die Jäger der ›Graf Zeppelin‹)*

sharply pulled up. At that moment one parachute popped open and got hung on the bomber's ventral ball turret."[41]

Another Fortress that failed to return was a B-17G (s/n 42-31377) of the 327th Bomb Squadron, 92nd Bomb Group, flown by 2/Lt. William R. Lavies. Its entire crew of ten successfully bailed out. Nine were taken prisoner, but unfortunately the commander, 2/Lt. Lavies, drowned in Limfjord. A third Fortress, a B-17G (s/n 42-31409) of the 364th Bomb Squadron, 305th Bomb Group, piloted by Lt. Charles O. Barnes was shot down over the sea, with the loss of its entire crew. A fourth bomber, a B-17G (s/n 42-31322) named "Mi Amigo" of the 364th Bomb Squadron, 305th Bomb Group, flown by Lt John G. Kriegshauser, suffered heavy combat damage during the attack of the Bf 109 Ts. Although it limped back to England, the aircraft crashed near Sheffield; everyone on board was killed. Heavy return fire claimed two Bf 109 T-2s (W.Nr. 7757 and W.Nr. 7732) and the lives of both pilots, Uffz. Erich Naujokat and Gefr. Kurt Schwarz.

Throughout March 1944 the Messerschmitt Bf 109 Ts of 11./JG 11 flew patrols in defense of coastal shipping. No successes were recorded in that period. On 30th March 1944, during a transfer flight from Liester to Mandal, Bf 109 T W.Nr. 7796 suffered engine failure. Its pilot, Uffz. Karl Tomanek, attempted to ditch the aircraft, but collided with a rock and was killed.

In Spring 1944, the remaining serviceable Bf 109 Ts continued their patrols along the coast of Norway. There were no encounters with the enemy in the air. By the end of May 1944 only one Bf 109 T still flew with the Staffel. The last machine of this type retired from operational service in late August 1944. Thus, the combat history of the Bf 109 T, the naval version of Willy Messerschmitt's most famous fighter design, came to an end.

The Bf 109 T is mentioned in the Luftwaffe's official records for the last time in a document dated 31st March 1945. The document was issued by Luftflotte 6 for the attention of the Luftwaffe High Command and discusses the possibility of obtaining additional fighter aircraft. They were needed urgently to provide cover for the evacuation fleet ferrying troops and civilians between the eastern and western part of the Baltic Sea. Luftflotte 6 was particularly interested in obtaining aircraft that could be launched from catapults mounted aboard ships travelling to Kurland. The catapult-launched fighters were to provide a means of defending the convoys against the Russian Air Force. Regular fighter cover by aircraft operating from land bases was impossible due to dwindling reserves of fuel and the general meagerness of the forces at hand. The Luftwaffe High Command produced the following reply:

"The Bf 109 T variant modified for catapult operations is no longer available. The Bf 109 variants currently in use weigh nearly 1,000 kg more, while the catapults were designed to handle Bf 109 Ts. Due to the present condition of our arms industry, designing a new catapult is not feasible. The same applies to the Fw 190. Presently, for the reasons mentioned above, there are no means to construct a suitable catapult."[42]

Bibliography

Marshall F.L., *Messerschmitt Bf 109 T, Die Jäger der ‚Graf Zeppelin'*, Dießen b.r.w.
Michulec R., *Messerschmitt Me 109, cz. 1*, Gdynia 1997
Murawski M.J., *Samoloty Luftwaffe 1933-1945, Tom II*, Warszawa 1997
Obermaier E., *Die Ritterkreuzträger der Luftwaffe, Jagdflieger 1939-1945*, Mainz 1966

Prien J., Rodeike P., *Jagdgeschwader 1 und 11, Teil 1: 1939-1943*, Eutin b.r.w.
Prien J., Stemmer G., Rodeike P. i Bock W., *Die Jagdfliegerverbände der Deutschen Luftwaffe 1934 bis 1945, Teil 5*, Eutin b.r.w.

Endnotes

[1] (Ger. *der Wetterfrosch*): in the Luftwaffe's vernacular, the meteorological officer (author's note).
[2] Two pairs of fighters, flying in "finger-four" formation, very much like an American flight (author's note).
[3] Flight leader and his wingman (author's note).
[4] The Luftwaffe's name for a defensive formation flown by American four-engined bombers: in the USAAF known as the 'combat box' (author's note).
[5] Popular nickname for the Bf 109 T amongst Luftwaffe pilots (author's note).
[6] Marshall F.L., *Messerschmitt Bf 109 T, Die Jäger der ‚Graf Zeppelin'*, Dießen, pp. 236-237.
[7] This code lettering, known as the *Stammkennzeichen*, was officially introduced in October 1939. The four letters identified each aircraft from the moment it left the factory until it was issued to a frontline unit. The code was usually painted on both sides of the fuselage, sometimes also on the wing undersurfaces.
[8] Aircraft carrier translates to German as *Flugzeugträger*, usually shortened to *Träger*.
[9] Approx. 262 meters (author's note).
[10] A naval version of the Supermarine Spitfire, adapted for operations from aircraft carriers (author's note).
[11] Marshall..., op. cit., pp. 49-50.
[12] In the 1980s Norwegian divers recovered parts of the aircraft's fuselage from the seabed.
[13] Dornier Do 24, a three-engined flying boat operated by the Luftwaffe (author's note).
[14] Marshall, *op. cit*., pp. 103-104.
[15] Codename for the ground control operator (author's note).
[16] Marshall..., *op. cit*., pp. 113-114.
[17] *Ibidem*, *op. cit*., pp. 128-129.
[18] On 27th December 1941, I./JG 77 participated in an action against a British landing at Vagsoy. German pilots claimed five victories on that day. However, at that time the I. Gruppe probably no longer had Bf 109 Ts on strength, operating only Bf 109 E-7s.
[19] A single-engined night fighter unit.
[20] Marshall..., *op. cit*., p. 195.
[21] HSS, Herausschuß – a practice recognized by the Luftwaffe of damaging a heavy bomber enough to force it out of a defensive 'combat box' formation. A lone, separated bomber was usually easy prey for prowling fighters.
[22] Ground control station at Jever.
[23] Homeland Defense.
[24] Marshall..., *op. cit*., pp. 215-217.
[25] Ewald Herhold did not return to active service until March 1944. He was then assigned to 4./JG 11, and injured once again, but survived the war.
[26] Marshall..., *op. cit*., p. 225.
[27] Marshall..., *op. cit*., p. 241.
[28] Marshall..., *op. cit*., p. 229.
[29] Prien J., Rodeike P.,..., *op. cit*., p. 364.
[30] Marshall..., *op. cit*. p. 233.
[31] *Ibidem*, *op. cit*., p. 236.
[32] *Dicke Auto* (a furniture van) – in the Luftwaffe's vernacular a four-engined bomber (author's note).
[33] Prien J., Rodeike P.,..., *op. cit*., pp. 387-389.
[34] Of the 549th Bomb Squadron / 385th Bomb Group (translator's note).
[35] Of the 548th Bomb Squadron / 385th Bomb Group (translator's note).
[36] Marshall..., *op. cit*., p. 241.
[37] Prien J., Rodeike P.,..., *op. cit*., p. 409.
[38] Marshall..., *op. cit*., p. 250.
[39] The day before they had been transferred from the island to the mainland.
[40] Marshall..., *op. cit*., p. 289.
[41] *Ibidem*, *op. cit*., p. 294.
[42] *Ibidem*, *op. cit*., p. 318.

Messerschmitt Bf 109 T

arkusz/Sheet 01

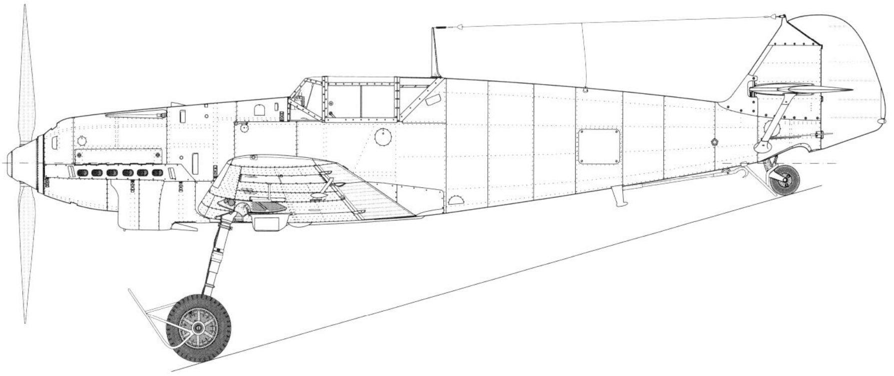

Bf 109 V17, W.Nr 1776, D-IYMS - Summer 1939,
Travemünde - port/ widok z lewej

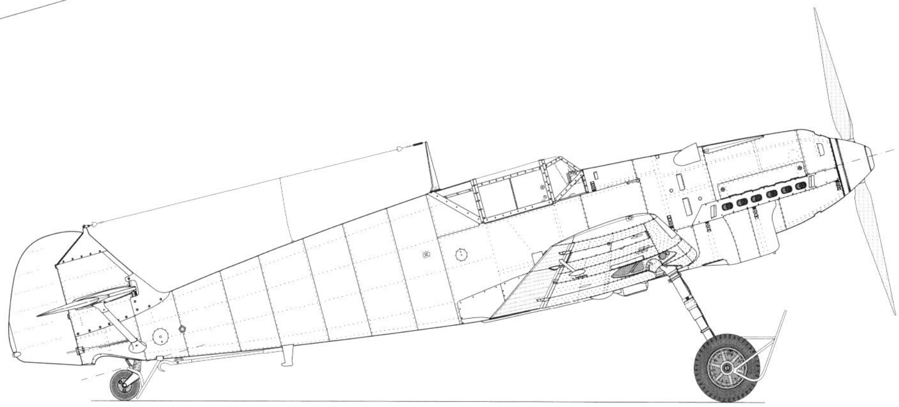

Bf 109 V17 - starboard/widok z prawej

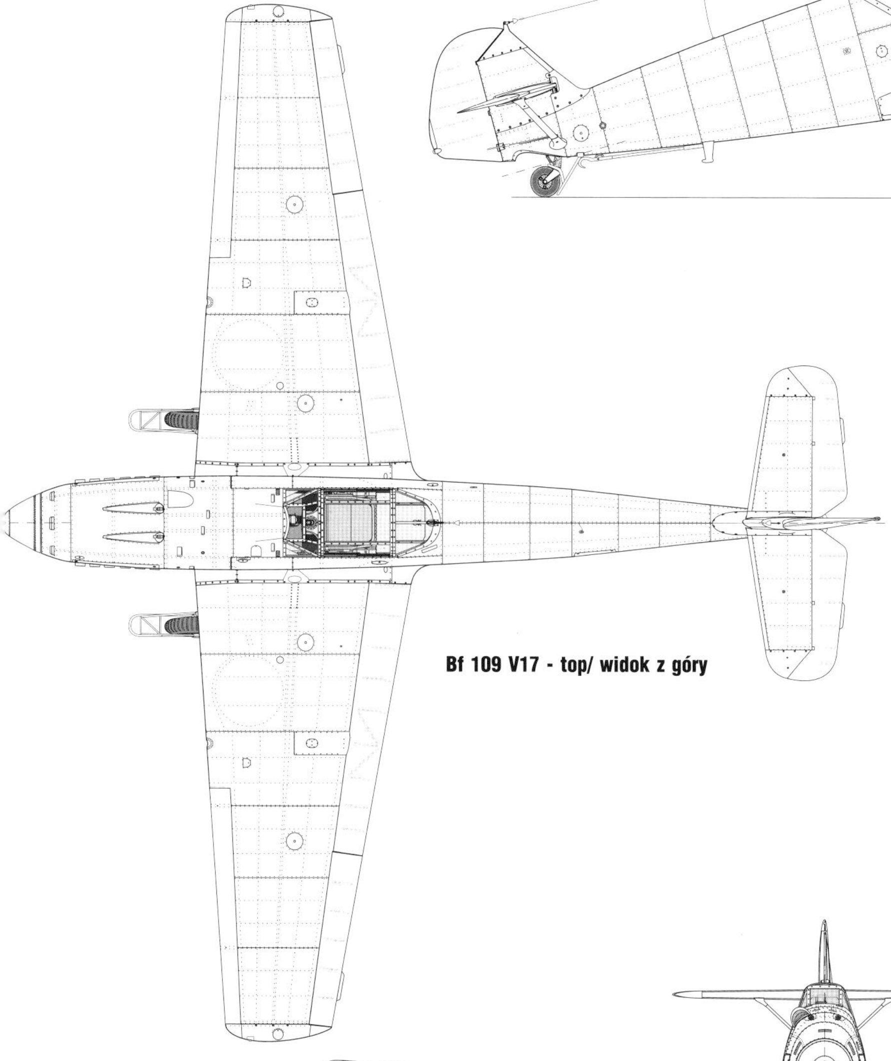

Bf 109 V17 - top/ widok z góry

Attention!
- In some views the course of riveted joints have been simplified for the drawings clearness
  Uwaga!
- Na części rzutów pominięto dla czytelności niektóre szwy nitowe

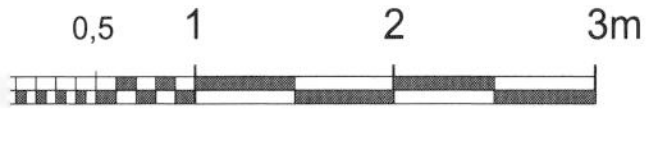

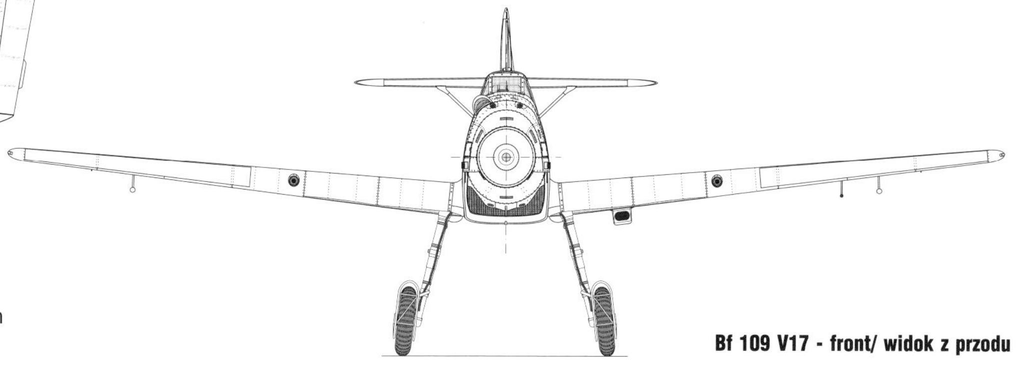

Bf 109 V17 - front/ widok z przodu

0,5 1 2 3m

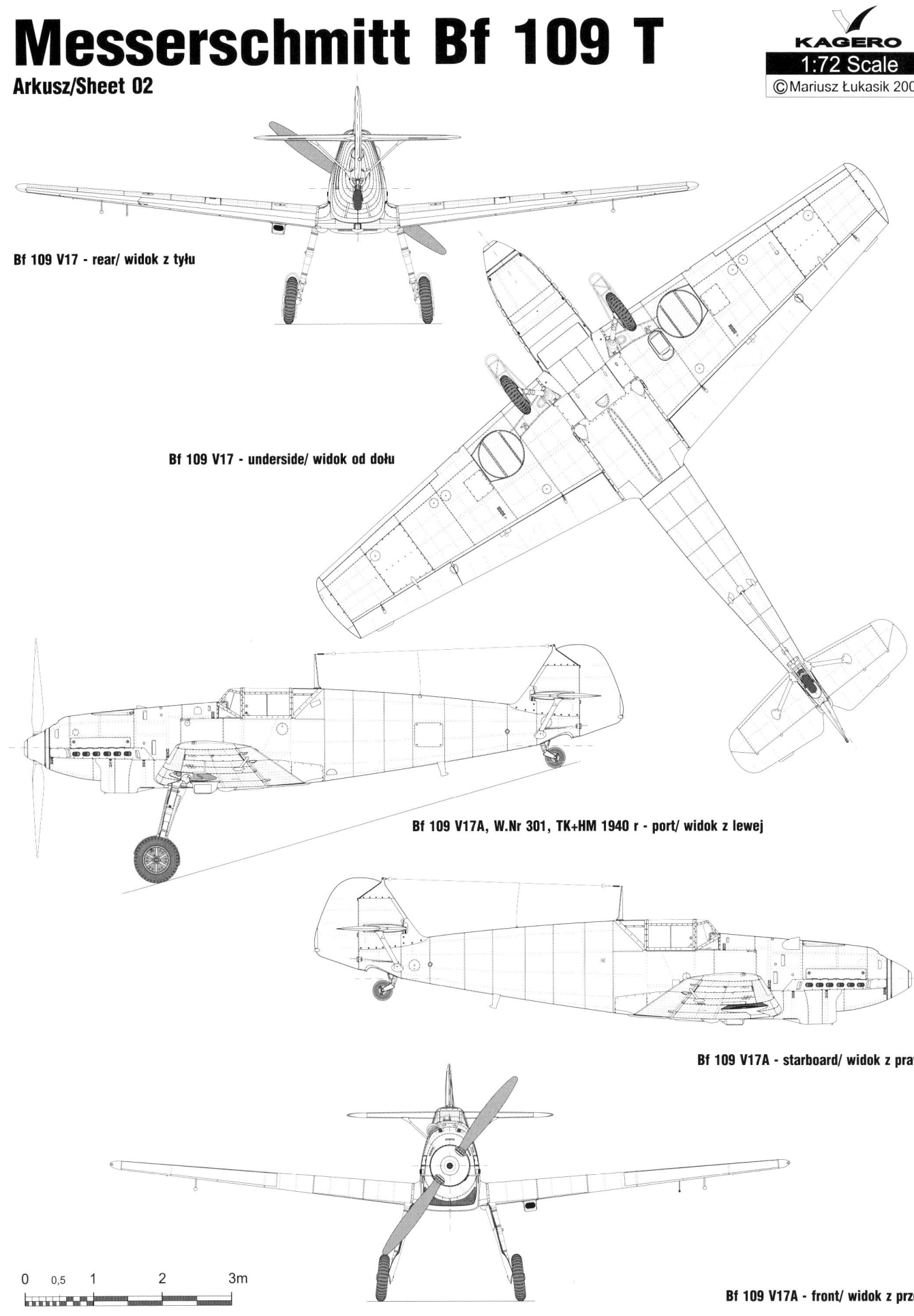

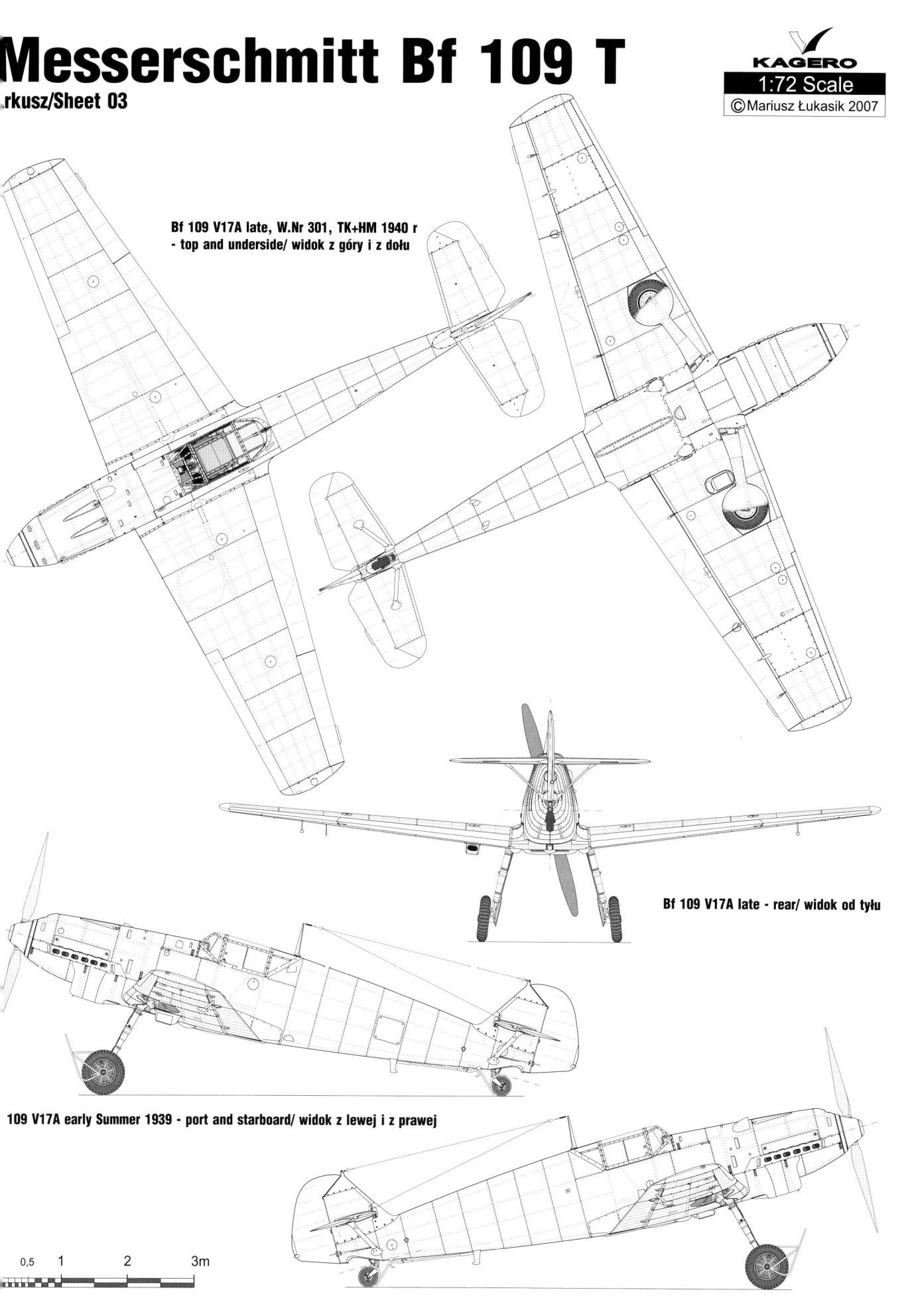

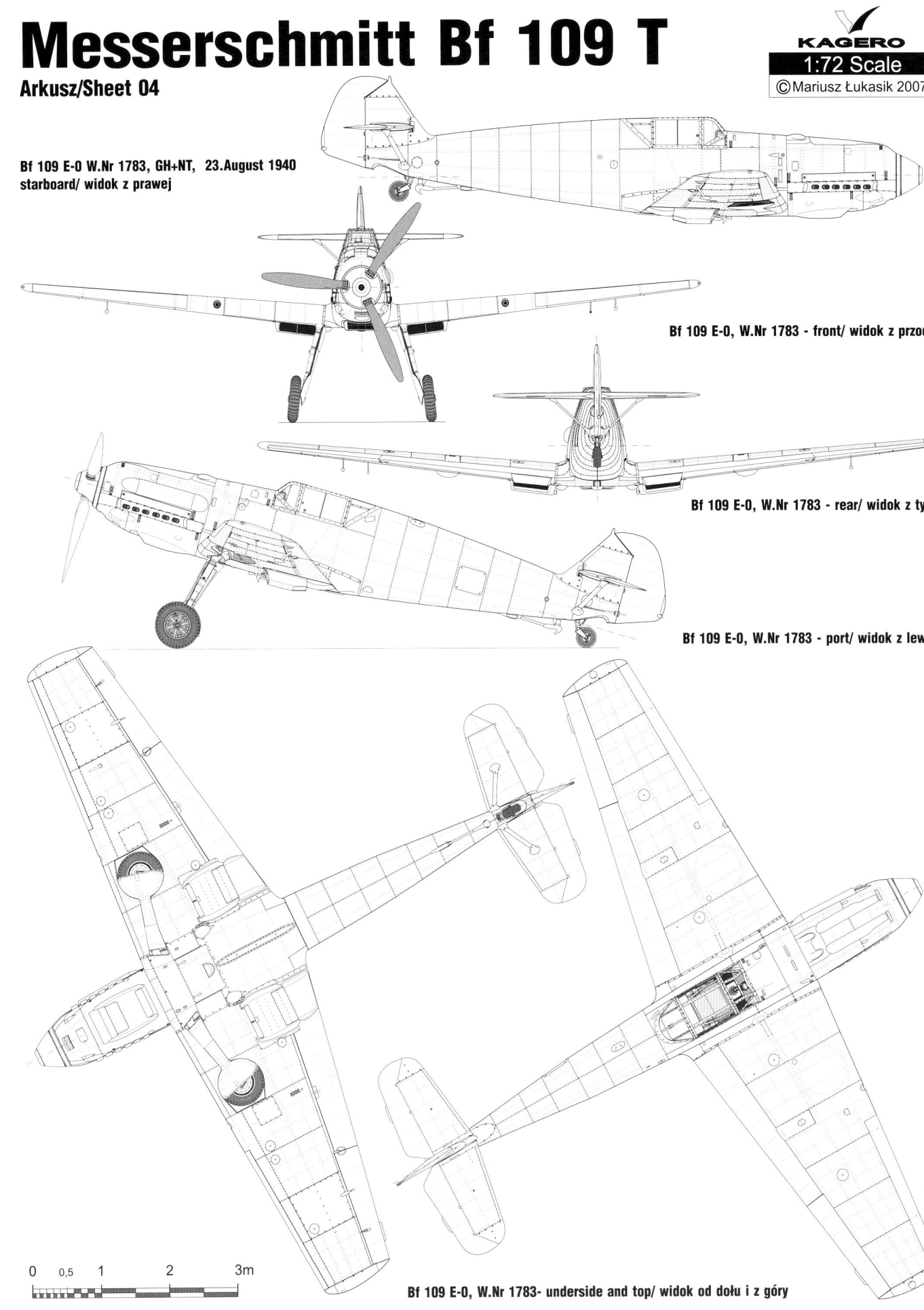

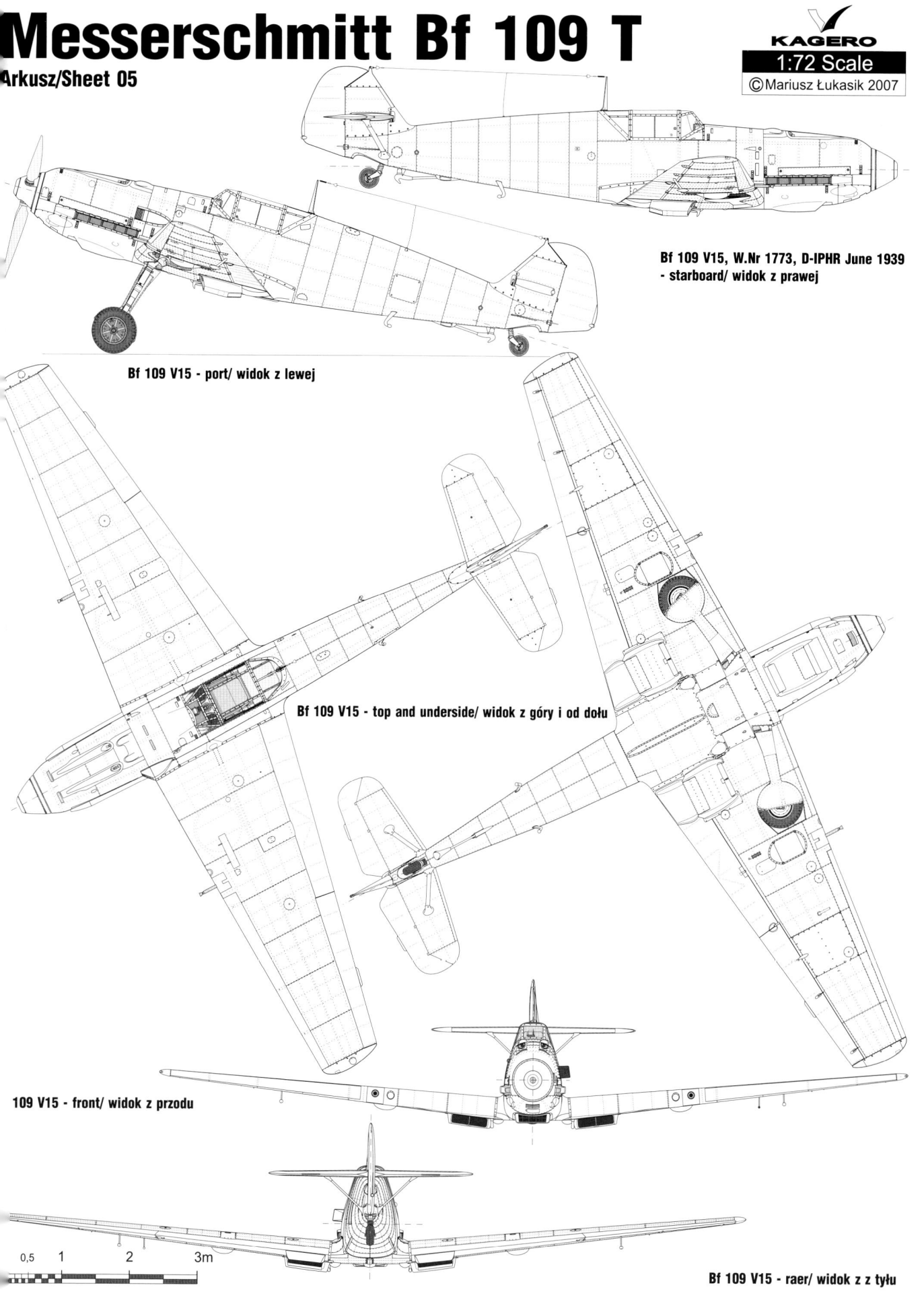

Messerschmitt Bf 109 T

Arkusz/Sheet 06

1:72 Scale
©Mariusz Łukasik 2007

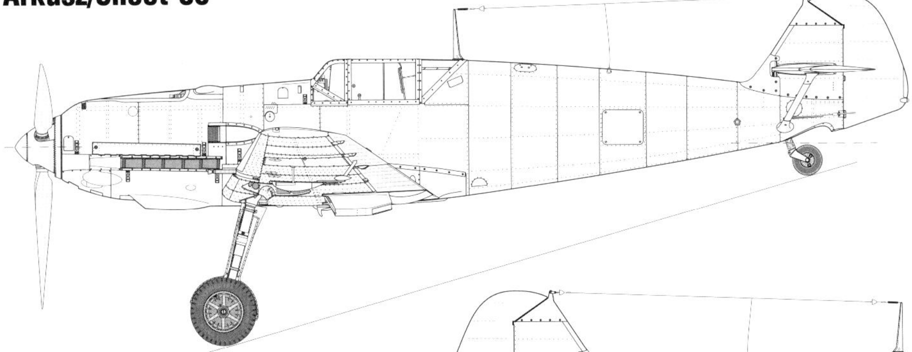

Bf 109 T-2 - port/ widok z lewej

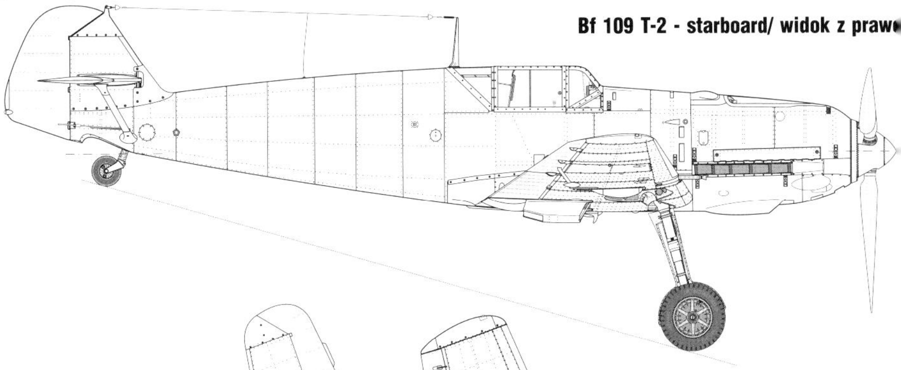

Bf 109 T-2 - starboard/ widok z prawej

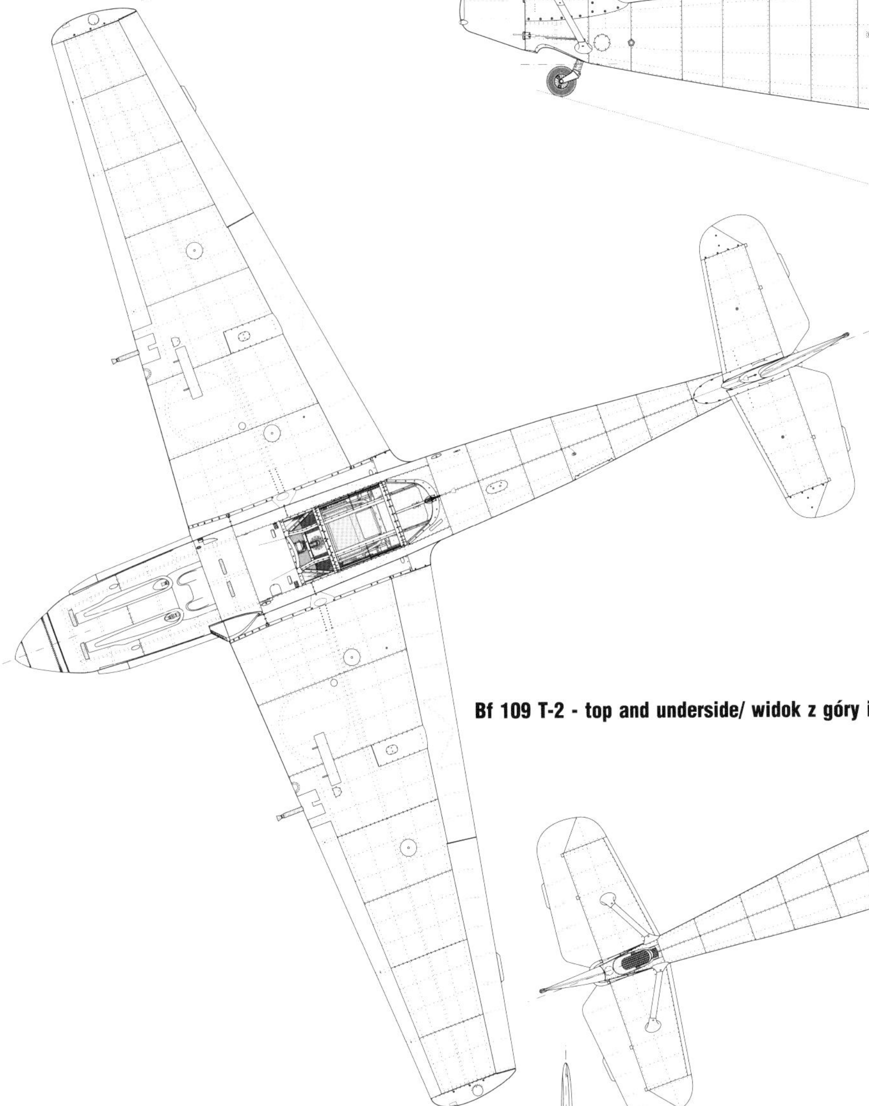

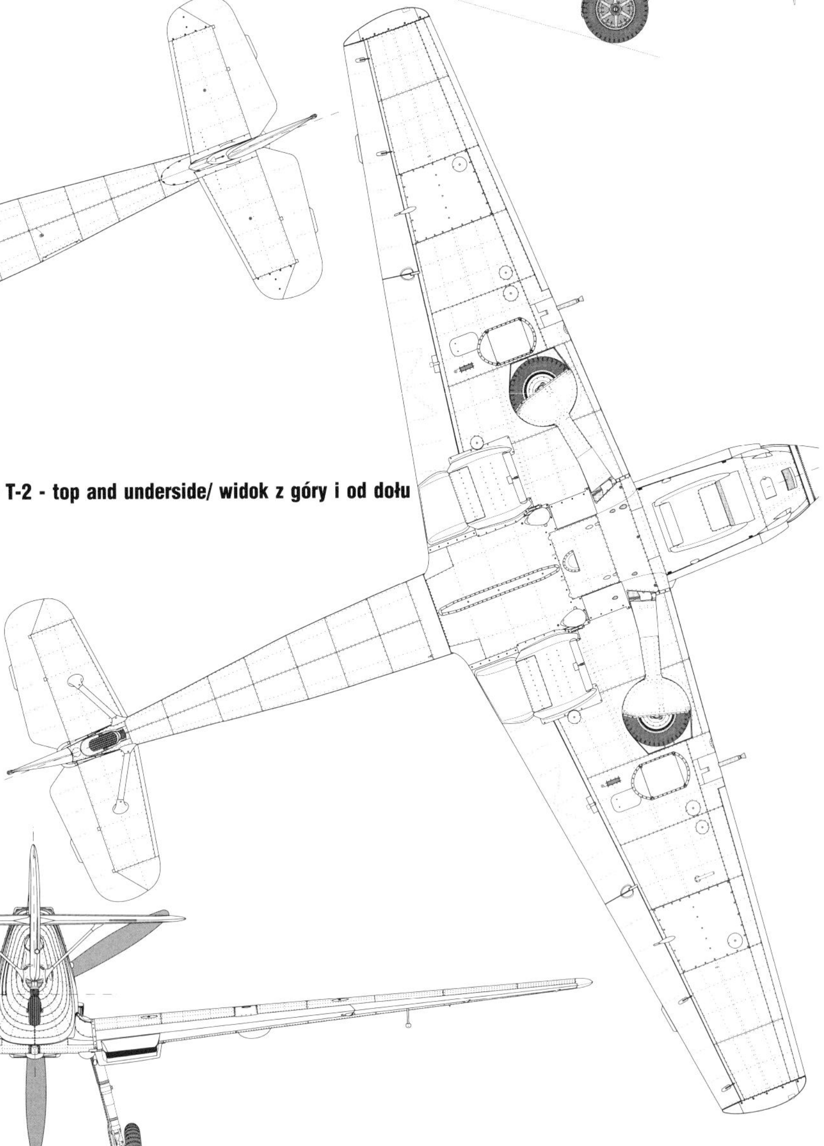

Bf 109 T-2 - top and underside/ widok z góry i od dołu

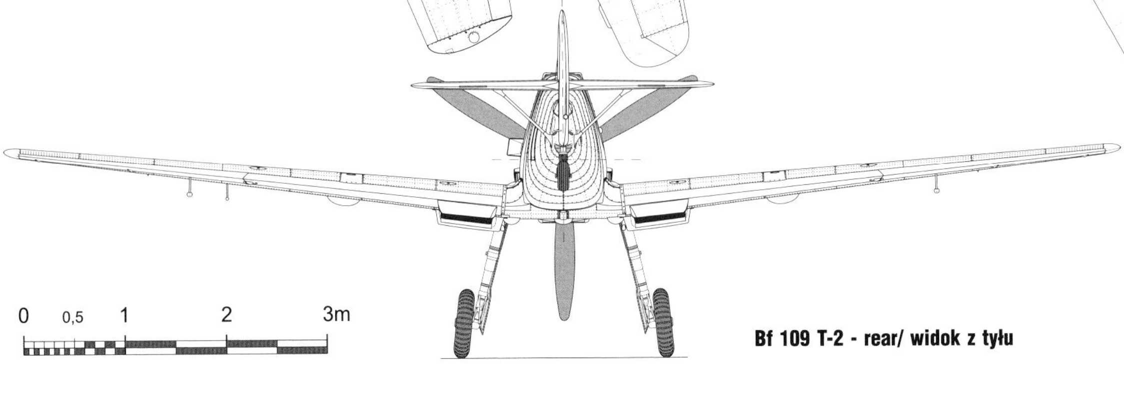

Bf 109 T-2 - rear/ widok z tyłu

0 0,5 1 2 3m

Messerschmitt Bf 109 T

Arkusz/Sheet 07

KAGERO
1:72 Scale
© Mariusz Łukasik 2007

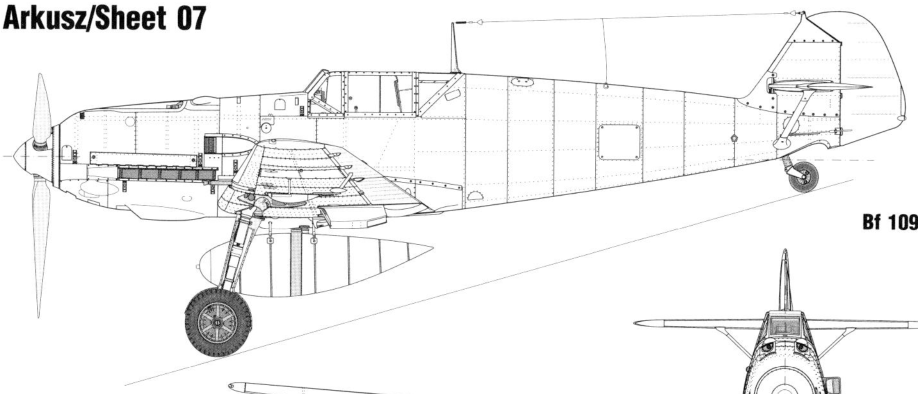

Bf 109 T-2 with 300 liter drop tank - port/ widok z lewej

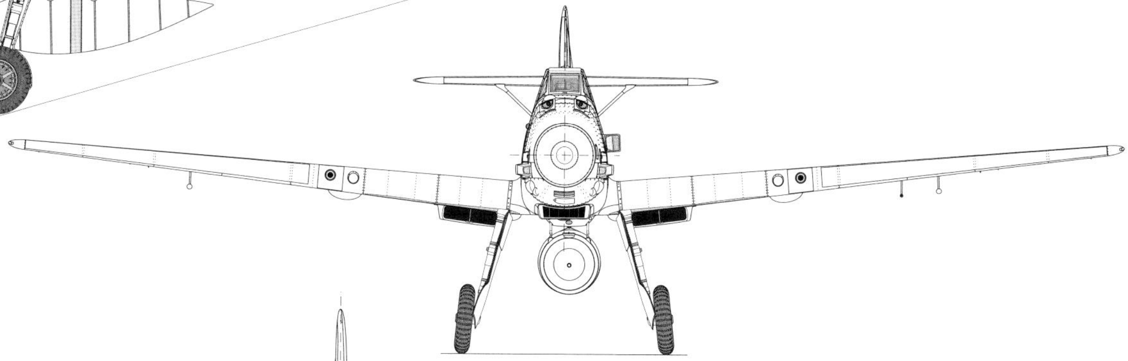

Bf 109 T-2 with 300 liter drop tank - front/ widok z przodu

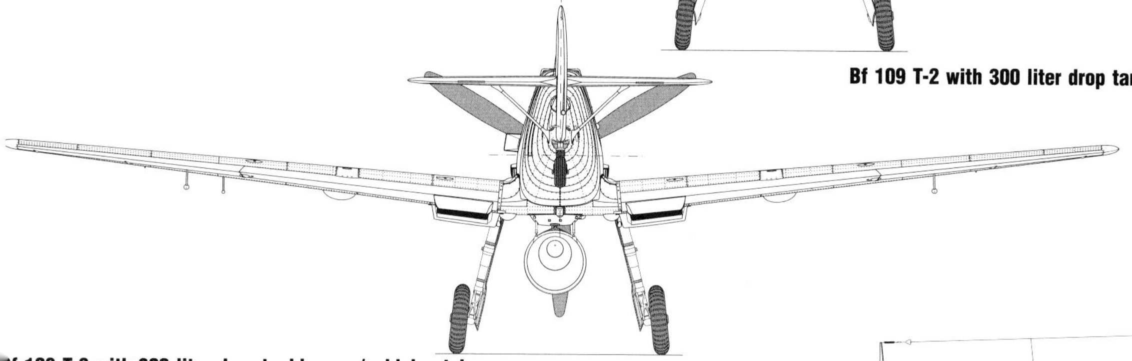

Bf 109 T-2 with 300 liter drop tankl - rear/ widok z tyłu

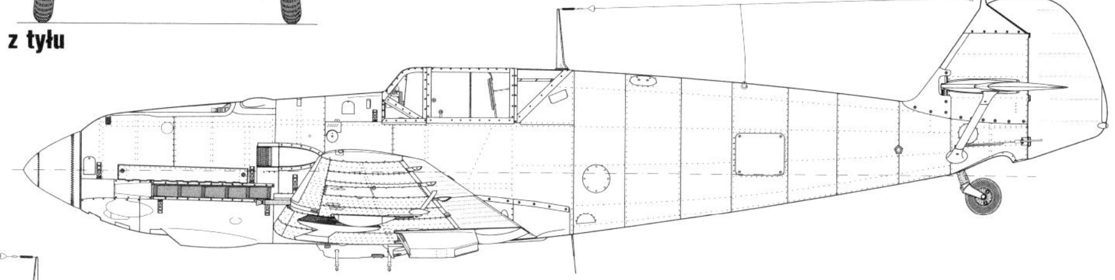

Bf 109 T-2 with FuG 25 - port/ widok z lewej

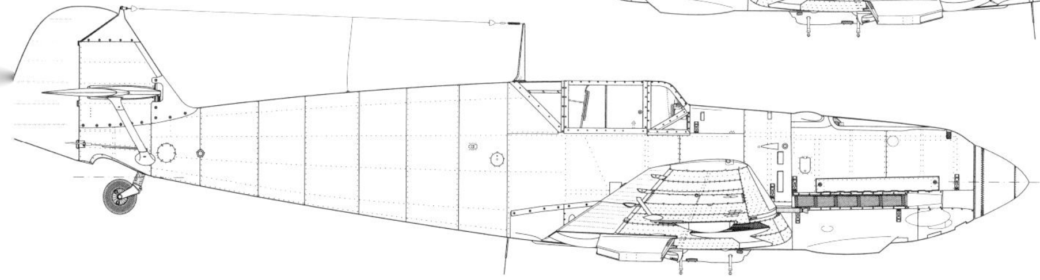

Bf 109 T-2 with FuG 25 - starboard/ widok z prawej

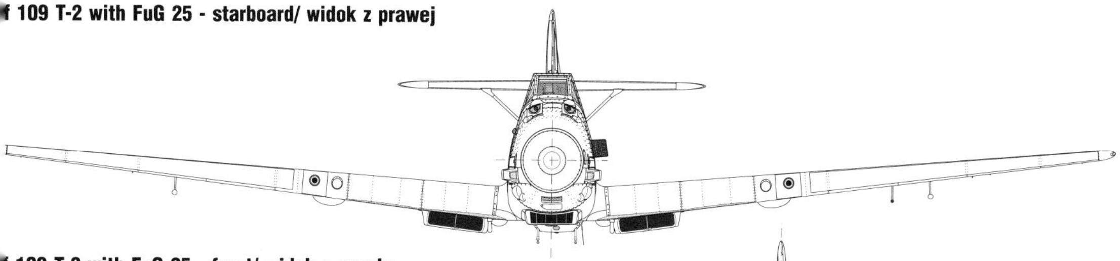

Bf 109 T-2 with FuG 25 - front/ widok z przodu

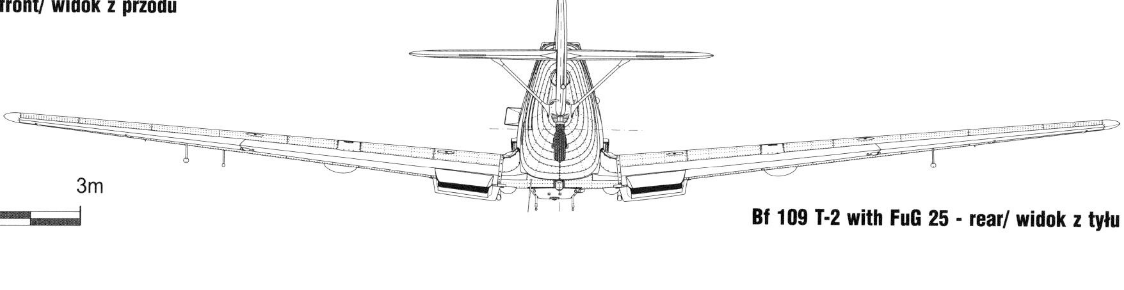

Bf 109 T-2 with FuG 25 - rear/ widok z tyłu

0,5 1 2 3m

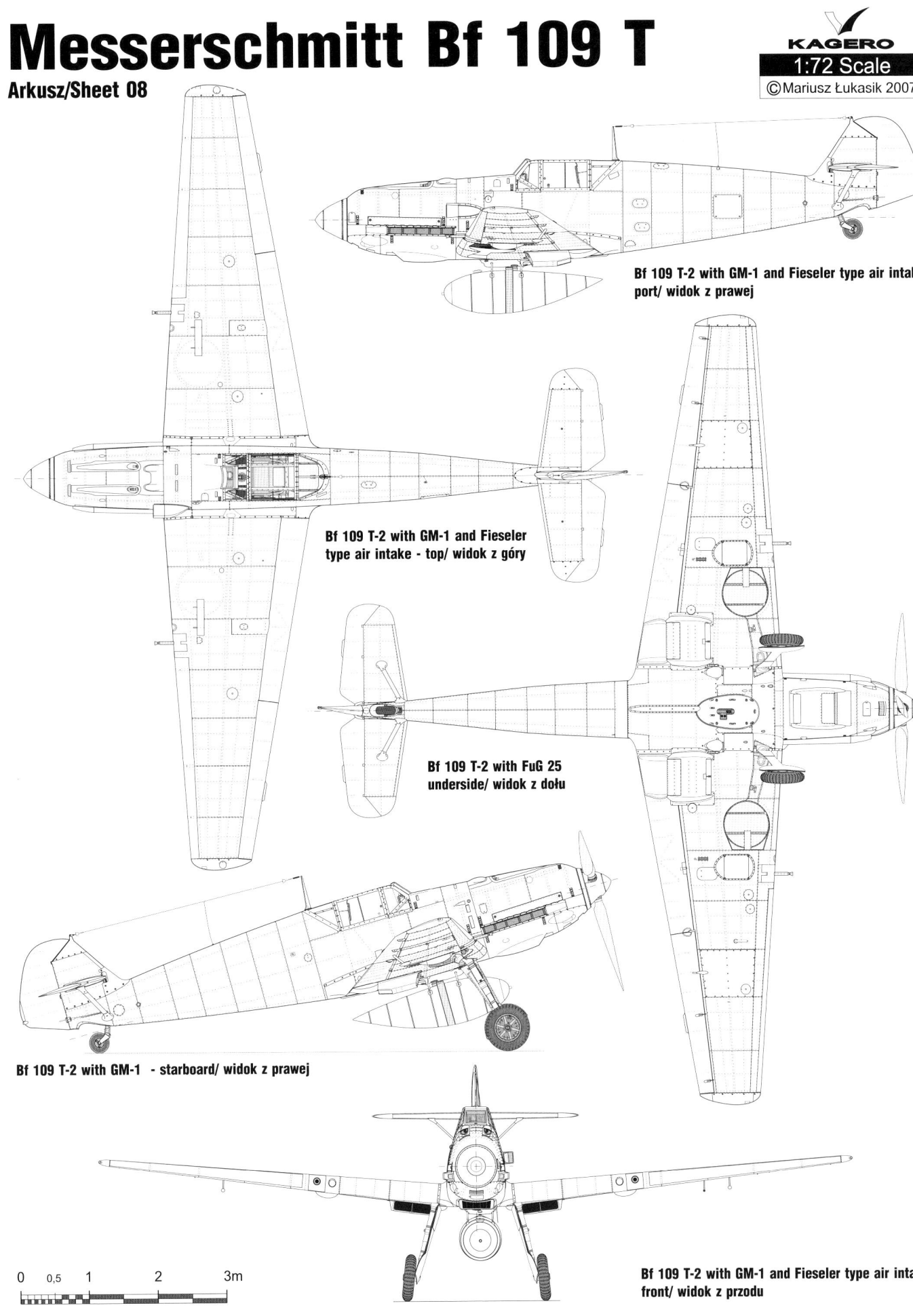

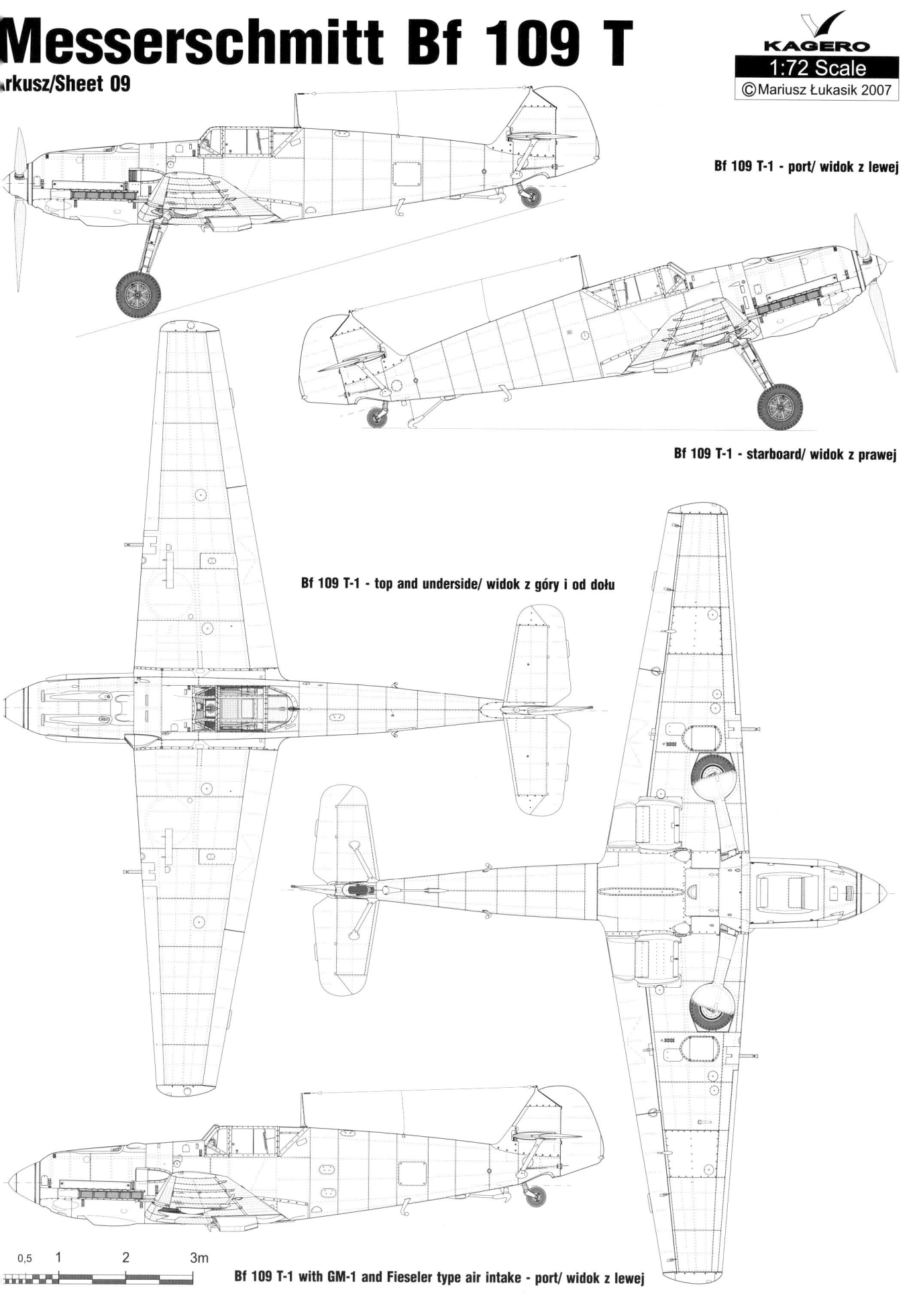

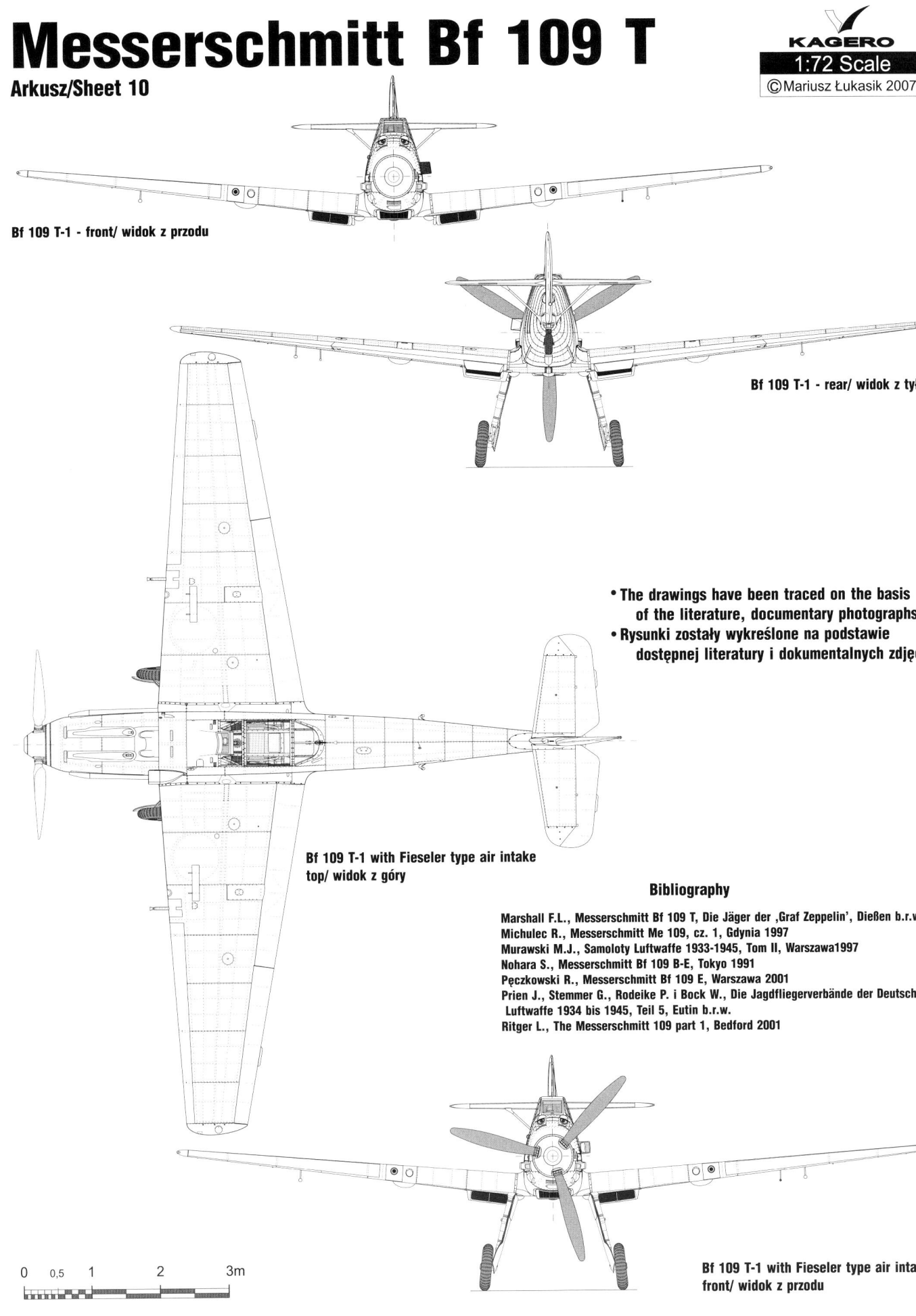

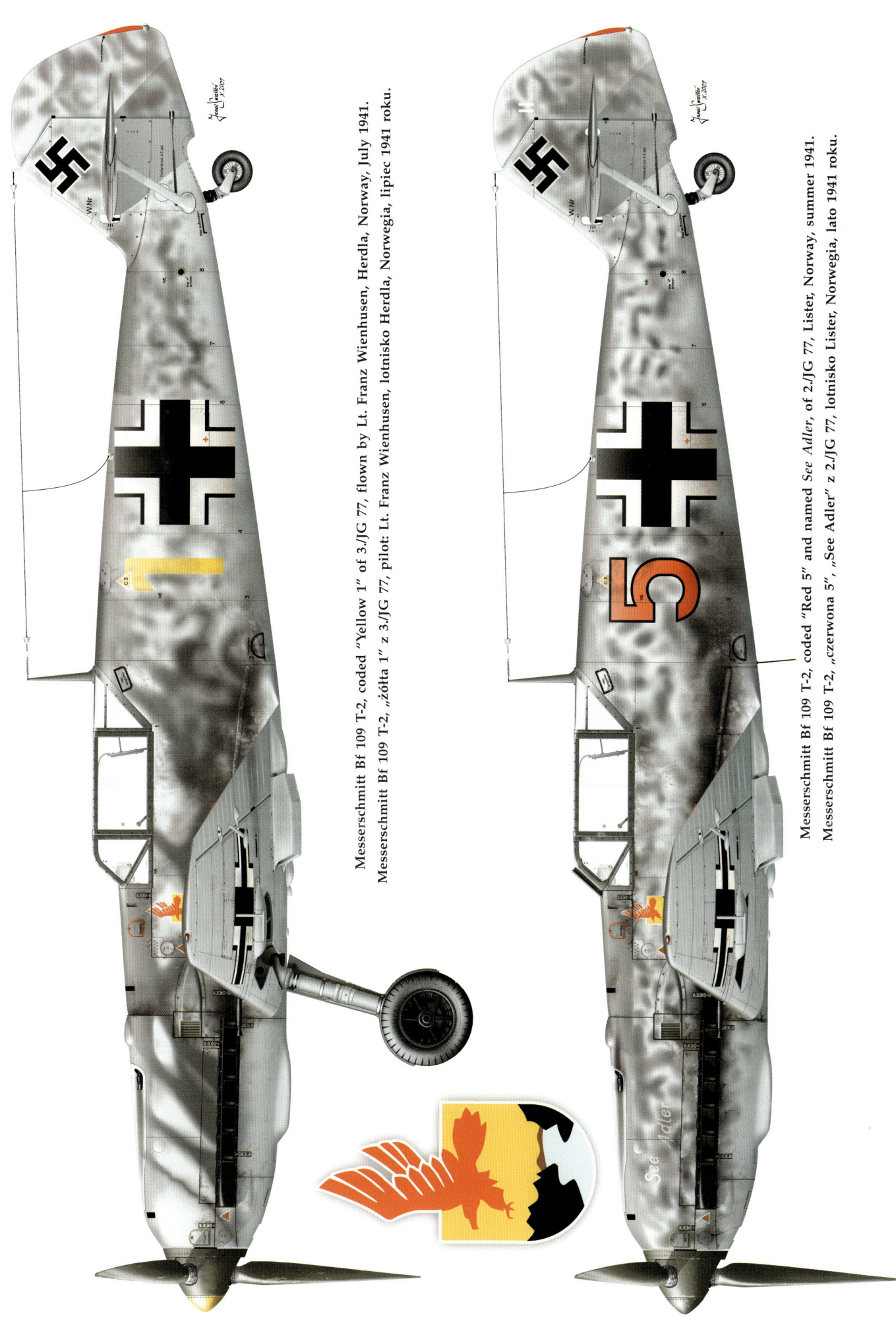

Messerschmitt Bf 109 T-2, coded "Yellow 1" of 3./JG 77, flown by Lt. Franz Wienhusen, Herdla, Norway, July 1941.
Messerschmitt Bf 109 T-2, „żółta 1" z 3./JG 77, pilot: Lt. Franz Wienhusen, lotnisko Herdla, Norwegia, lipiec 1941 roku.

Messerschmitt Bf 109 T-2, coded "Red 5" and named See Adler, of 2./JG 77, Lister, Norway, summer 1941.
Messerschmitt Bf 109 T-2, „czerwona 5", „See Adler" z 2./JG 77, lotnisko Lister, Norwegia, lato 1941 roku.

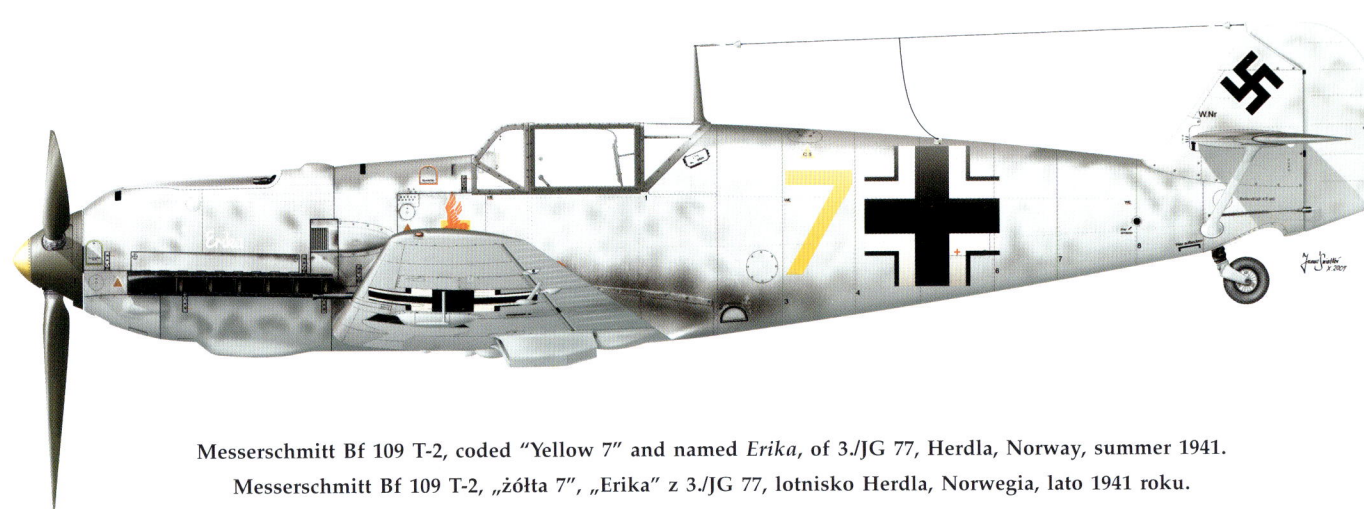

Messerschmitt Bf 109 T-2, coded "Yellow 7" and named *Erika*, of 3./JG 77, Herdla, Norway, summer 1941.
Messerschmitt Bf 109 T-2, „żółta 7", „Erika" z 3./JG 77, lotnisko Herdla, Norwegia, lato 1941 roku.

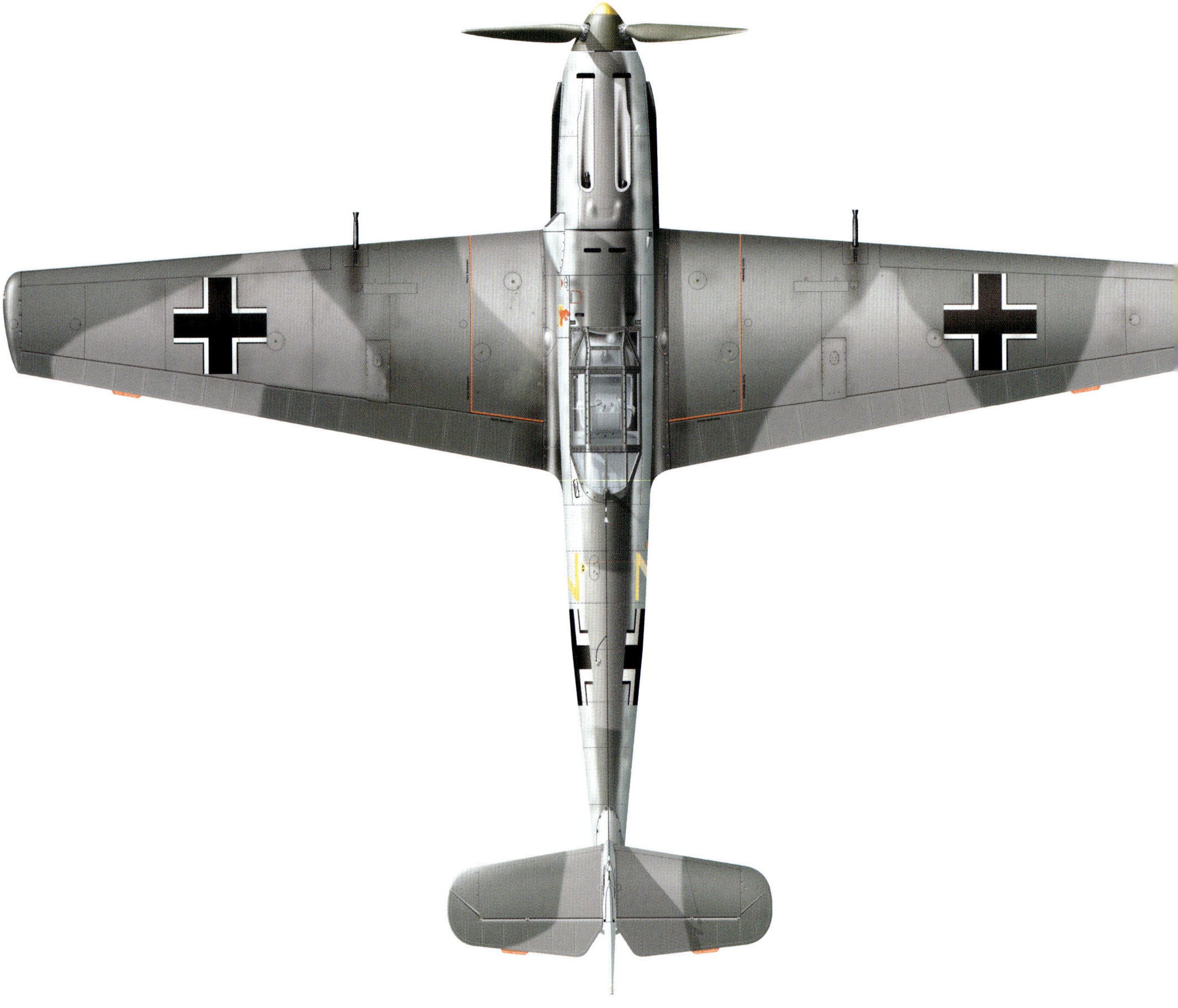

Messerschmitt Bf 109 T-2, coded "Yellow 7" and named *Erika*, of 3./JG 77, top view.
The camouflage is typical of aircraft W.Nr. 7728 through 7743.

Messerschmitt Bf 109 T-2, „żółta 7", „Erika" z 3./JG 77, rzut z góry kamuflażu typowego dla samolotów o numerach seryjnych od W.Nr. 7728 do 7743.

Messerschmitt Bf 109 T-2, coded "White 5" of Jagdgruppe Drontheim, Trondheim-Vaernes, Norway, summer 1941.
Messerschmitt Bf 109 T-2, „biała 5" z Jagdgruppe Drontheim, lotnisko Trondheim-Vaernes, Norwegia, lato 1941 roku.

Messerschmitt Bf 109 T-2, "White 4" of 13./JG 77, flown by Lt. Alfred Jakobi, Stavanger-Sola, Norway, September 1941.
Messerschmitt Bf 109 T-2, „biała 4" z 13./JG 77, pilot: Lt. Alfred Jakobi, lotnisko Stavanger-Sola, Norwegia, wrzesień 1941 roku.

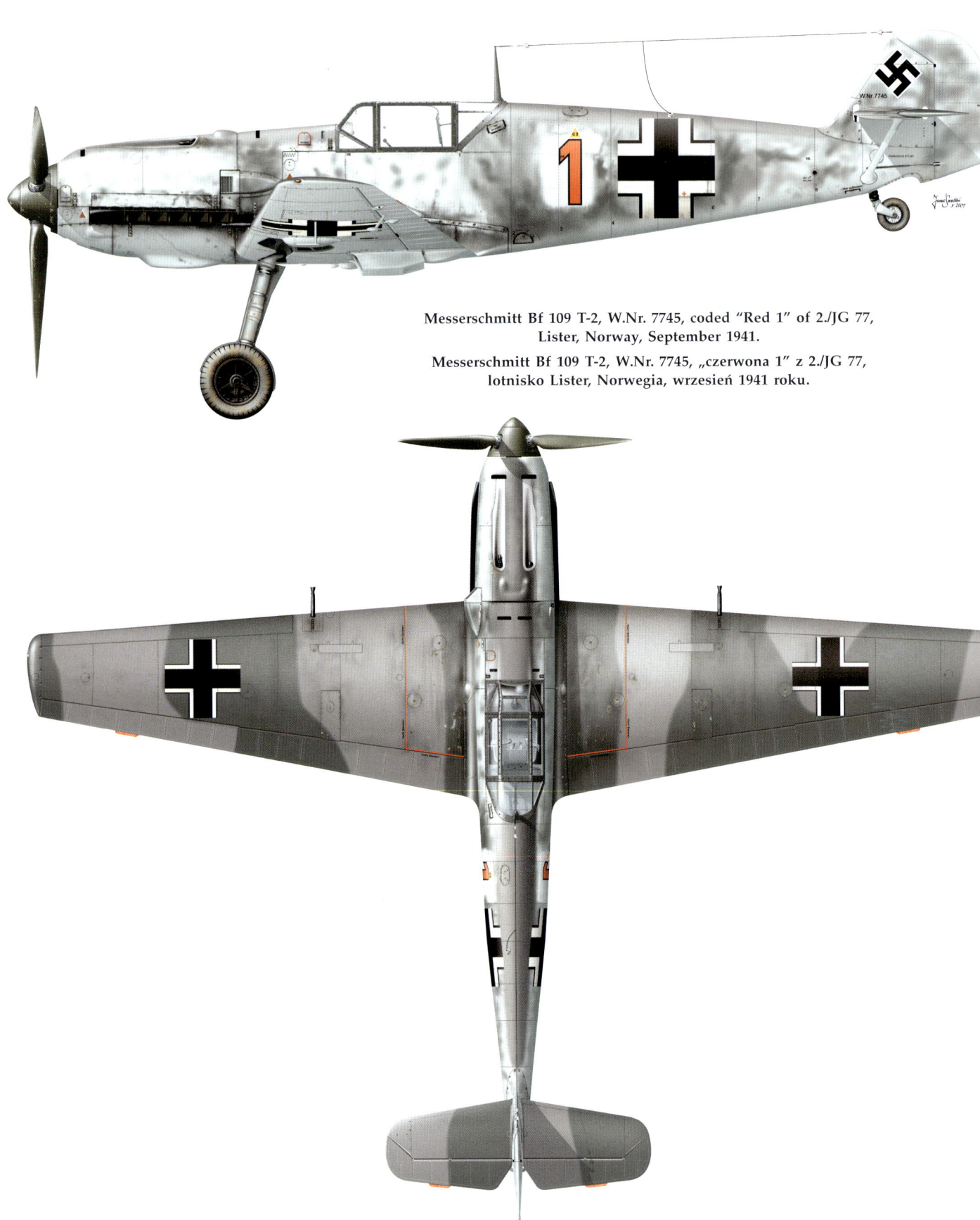

Messerschmitt Bf 109 T-2, W.Nr. 7745, coded "Red 1" of 2./JG 77, Lister, Norway, September 1941.

Messerschmitt Bf 109 T-2, W.Nr. 7745, „czerwona 1" z 2./JG 77, lotnisko Lister, Norwegia, wrzesień 1941 roku.

Messerschmitt Bf 109 T-2, W.Nr. 7745, coded "Red 1" of 2./JG 77, top view. The camouflage is typical of aircraft W.Nr. 7744 through 7797.

Messerschmitt Bf 109 T-2, W.Nr. 7745, „czerwona 1" z 2./JG 77, rzut z góry kamuflażu typowego dla samolotów o numerach seryjnych od W.Nr. 7744 do 7797.